Subjectivity and Method in Psychology

*G*ender and *P*sychology

Series editor: Sue Wilkinson

This international series provides a forum for the growing body of distinctively psychological research focused on gender issues. While work on the psychology of women, particularly that adopting a feminist perspective, will be central, the series will also reflect other emergent trends in the field of gender. It will encourage contributions which are critical of the mainstream of androcentric or 'gender-neutral' psychology but also innovative in their suggested alternatives.

The books will explore topics where gender is central, such as social and sexual relationships, employment, health and illness, and the development of gender identity. Issues of theory and methodology raised by the study of gender in psychology will also be addressed.

The objective is to present research on gender in the context of its broader implications for psychology. These implications include the need to develop theories and methods appropriate to studying the experience of women as well as men, and working towards a psychology which reflects the experiences and concerns of both sexes.

The series will appeal to students of psychology, women's studies and gender studies and to professionals concerned with gender issues in their practice, as well as to the general reader with an interest in gender and psychology.

Sue Wilkinson is principal lecturer and head of the psychology section at Coventry Polytechnic.

Also in this series

Feminists and Psychological Practice
edited by Erica Burman

Feminist Groupwork
Self, Identity and Change
Sandra Butler and Claire Wintram

Subjectivity and Method in Psychology

Gender, Meaning and Science

Wendy Hollway

SAGE Publications

London · Newbury Park · New Delhi

SAGE Publications Ltd
28 Banner Street
London EC1Y 8QE

SAGE Publications Inc
275 South Beverly Drive
Beverly Hills, California 90212

SAGE Publications India Pvt Ltd
32, M-Block Market
Greater Kailash - I
New Delhi 110 048

British Library Cataloguing in Publication data

Hollway, Wendy, *1949–*
  Subjectivity and method in psychology:
  gender, meaning and science. – (Gender and psychology)
  1. Psychology. Research. Methodology
  I. Title   II. Series
  150′.72

  ISBN 0–8039–8207–0
  ISBN 0–8039–8209–9 Pbk

Library of Congress catalog card number 89–60458

Typeset by The Word Shop, Haslingden, Rossendale,
Lancashire

Printed in Great Britain by Billing and Sons Ltd,
Worcester

Contents

To my mother and my daughter

Acknowledgements

I would like to thank Valerie Walkerdine and Evelyn Fox Keller, who read parts of the manuscript for this book, and Sue Wilkinson, whose thorough comments at various stages have improved the final product. Thanks especially to Robin Lister, who not only read through an early draft with a keen editorial eye, but provided me with the time and space to write and encouraged me throughout.

Wendy Hollway

Introduction

This is a book about how a research method can escape the limitations of what is acceptable in psychology, why it needs to do so and what this involves for developing new theory too. It gives an account of how I evolved a method and theory which was adequate to the psychological research I wanted to conduct about gender identity, research which was inspired by my own and others' experiences during times of change. In 1982 I was awarded a Ph.D. in psychology for the research entitled 'Identity and Gender Difference in Adult Social Relations'. Five years after completing the thesis, I have finally found time to write this book which, although it is based on the thesis, has a different focus. The Ph.D. thesis has been in demand, partly because it provides a radically different theory of gender, but mainly because it provides a model of psychological method which actually addresses the complex questions that people often go into psychology to understand better: questions about themselves and those they know; questions of identity and the hidden sources of their conduct; questions of relationships, power, dependence and change.

Standard psychological methods – not just experimental ones, but in a different way humanistic ones – transform such questions until we lose touch with what it was we wanted to know, or why. But these are not just limitations of method, since methods are accompanied by theoretical assumptions about the individual. I have come to believe that the way psychology keeps theory and method separate is a serious contributory factor to its problems. This book is about method, but in discussing method, it constantly keeps in view the theoretical requirements for an alternative. Therefore, in the first part of the book, I describe my method and what enabled me to develop it. My method was based on participants' accounts of their experiences explored through unstructured dialogues and group discussions loosely based on the principles of consciousness-raising. Two sets of conditions contributed primarily to its development: experiences outside my academic life, in particular the women's movement, and theoretical developments outside psychology which provided me with the means of conducting a thoroughgoing critique of psychology's assumptions.

In the middle section of the book, I deal with the theoretical precepts which enabled me to analyse the interview material according to what I call interpretative discourse analysis. It provides

a way of understanding subjectivity within discourses and power relations which can explain gender difference. After an introduction to the
debates within which new concepts are situated, I introduce the necessary concepts entirely through extracts from participants' accounts.

In the last part of the book I bring the focus back to psychology as a
science. My approach, rather than treating psychology as objective
science, is to look at the conditions which produced the various
strands of psychological knowledge. I apply this approach to feminist
social psychology in the hope of understanding what might undermine its emancipatory intentions. Finally, I apply my theory of
subjectivity and gender to the question of the role of masculinity in
producing psychology as we know it. With this I come back round to
an issue posed by my research: under what conditions can women do
different psychology?

During the period leading up to and during my thesis work, I was
doing a variety of things which were relevant to my understanding of
self and others; writing a journal, recording my dreams, being a
member of women's consciousness-raising groups, teaching group
dynamics through experiential methods and, above all, talking endlessly to friends – about them and about me. Gradually I found a
place in my research for these experiences and what I was learning
from them. Yet as someone trained in psychology, employed as a
teacher of psychology and wanting to address these questions within
the framework of a Ph.D. in psychology, I expected to exclude them.
I expected to be able to start from the concepts and methods of
psychology. This could have been the end of my search. Without the
support of other practices and sets of ideas I would have ended up
doing a Ph.D. on sex-role stereotyping or (what was very progressive
at the time) on androgyny, using methods developed within the
requirements of statistical data analysis. Such research would have
undermined my initial intentions by reducing the phenomena I
experienced to those amenable to measurement and trivializing
gender until I could no longer have made connections between
psychological knowledge and my knowledge outside that realm.

I became a student of psychology in 1968 and over the last two
decades I have often been confronted with the problem of how I
represent 'being a psychologist' to lay people. I wanted to study
psychology because I wanted to understand people (that phrase has
come to sound trite and naive, but I think it needs to be reclaimed for
serious psychology). My interest came out of a family tradition
(matrilineal) in which both my mother and grandmother were forever being called upon to listen and help sort out people's problems.
By the time I graduated my standard response to people who, on
learning that I was studying psychology, said 'oh you must be able to

read my mind' or some such comment, had become to deny that I knew any more about people than anyone else. I held to this position for a long time. Meanwhile, outside academic work I learned more about myself and other people, and as I became someone to whom people chose to talk about themselves and their relationships, I made the distinction between 'psychology' and what I understood about people. Being employed as a teacher of applied social psychology faced me starkly with the discrepancy.

My employment as a psychologist has enabled me to have the time and resources to inquire into people's psychology and in this way has helped me to understand much about the reasons for people's conduct. I regarded this as common understanding until I realized how many people are without it. Yet when I make one of my occasional visits to the periodicals shelves in psychology libraries, or check the most recent textbooks, I am reminded that what I know bears little or no resemblance to psychology as a discipline. I still do not know how to respond to those who assume that psychology has taught me to understand people. Except that by running the risk of doing an unorthodox Ph.D., and by writing this book, I hope to show how a psychology which understands people is possible.

Being a Woman

In what sense did being a woman affect how I went about my research? In the context of this series on *Gender and Psychology*, it is an important question, and one which is implicit throughout the book. I hope by the end to have applied the concepts I initially developed in order to understand gender difference in heterosexual relations to the issue of gender in psychological research. It is an area fraught with difficulty and yet politically important in the context of the recent claim that women can research the psychology of women differently (or better) than men. There is no adequate account of how or why this is the case and so by default those who believe there is some truth in the claim end up landed with the assumption that women's difference is somehow natural. From the beginning of my research I was committed to understanding the ways in which gender is a social production. This means that I should be able to explain not only why and under what circumstances women can do psychology differently from men, but why and under what circumstances they do not. It should then also be possible to analyse why and under what circumstances men both do what they do and could do psychology differently. To help me to avoid falling into claims about women's difference being 'natural', in this case in psychological research, I try to understand what I did and why, and detail the conditions which made it possible. Before going on to that discussion I shall outline the theme of the book and how it develops.

The Contents of the Book
In this introduction, I try to explain how I came up with the questions I did and how they changed as I went along. It would be impossible to present these questions fully without talking about myself: the point that I was at in my life and aspects of its history, the cultural and political conditions that produced it, how these shaped my interest in certain areas of contemporary social theory. These factors together produced the conditions which made possible my research questions and shaped how I addressed them. The methods that I developed (what material I used or produced, how and why) are the subject of Chapter 1. I describe how I went about gathering material, and how this involved a continuous process of redefining acceptable psychological method. Throughout the process of data collection and analysis, I was evolving the theoretical framework which fed back to inform both my analysis of data and the way I generated material in discussions with participants. In Chapter 2 I set out the theoretical debates within which my work is situated and introduce the concepts on which it is based, concepts which can only be fully understood through repeated use in the analysis of material which takes place in the book.

Chapter 3 is concerned with the inadequacies of theories of meaning used in social scientific methods of interpreting accounts. I argue that the notion of 'women's experience' in feminist social psychology is subject to many of the same limitations in understanding meaning. I illustrate some of the methodological issues involved in interpreting a specific extract and suggest the utility of the idea of discourses and people's positioning in relation to them.

Chapters 4 and 5 are concerned with the theory required to analyse the accounts of self and experience given by participants and used as research data. I present and explain the theory in the course of using it on my own material. What psychological method lacks is a theory of how meaning is achieved; a theory which can be applied to understanding how accounts are produced and how they should be analysed. Chapter 4 outlines such a theory, using cases from my research to illustrate what I define as material, how I find or produce it and how I analyse it. I define three discourses concerning sexuality and illustrate how I use these to analyse subjectivity and social difference (in this case gender difference). A central idea is the differential power in different positions in discourses which are available to people on the basis of major categories of social difference. Chapter 5 provides the second major strand in an account of subjectivity. It takes the single case of Will and Beverley's relationship and looks at the psychodynamic processes which affect their relationship, their subjectivity and their gender difference. I use the concepts of defences against anxiety, projection and splitting (from Melanie Klein) to account for the processes involved in the reproduction of difference. I discuss the implications for method of this approach.

The purpose of Chapters 6 and 7 is to apply the theory to psychological method and to consider the implications for feminist psychology. I start by taking an historical approach. Chapter 6 looks at the conditions of emergence of orthodox psychological methods – pure, applied and humanistic – and the theories that accompany them. The review and critique of the literature in my thesis was based on the social psychology of sex roles and stereotyping and androgyny research with which I had fundamental disagreements. The field has moved on since then and feminist psychologists have mounted just such a critique (Sayers, 1986; Wetherell, 1986). So I couple that critique with a historical analysis in considering the new feminist social psychology (taking Sue Wilkinson's recent collection for my example). Chapter 7 starts with a discussion of research which argues for a relation between science and gender. On this basis I consider how gender difference might be implicated in psychological methods. I use the theory outlined in previous chapters to analyse the place of the researcher's subjectivity in the reproduction of psychological methods. I conclude by considering the implications of this understanding of the production of psychology for feminist and other psychologies with emancipatory goals.

The Thesis Questions
How is gender difference reproduced (and therefore also modified) in adult relations? It was a long time before I could even pose the question in this form. At a theoretical level, to get to this point I had to question four of the most fundamental assumptions of social psychology: the individual, childhood origins, socialization and stereotyping. My commitment to a theory which could account for my own changes led me from questions about the origins of sex differences (seen in terms of childhood socialization and the learning of sex or gender 'roles'). I moved to a perspective on what I called the recursive reproduction of gender difference in adult social relations. The focus on relations made it possible to define the question in terms of difference between genders, rather than in terms of women.

This change in basic tenets for a theory of gender difference was not easy or immediate; the alternative focus emerged gradually and intermittently throughout the data analysis. Several strands in my activities prior to the Ph.D., and which continued during it, enabled me to follow the transformation through. In the first place I was committed to accounting for personal change and resistances to it, rather than providing a scientific justification of the status quo (as for example I see sociobiologists doing in the sphere of gender), and available approaches in social psychology could not help. My political position was typical of the intellectual left in the 1970s in its concern with ideology and its criticism equally of economic and biological or psychological determinism. The idea of a politics of everyday life was also consistent with the new feminism, though not limited to it. These political positions were closely connected with the wave of new social theory emanating primarily from France, Germany and Italy – theories of ideology, structuralism, semiotics and developments in psychoanalysis – which was slow to have any bearing on psychology. I remember how excited I was to get hold of a pre-publication draft of the launch article of a new journal called *Ideology and Consciousness*, in which the members of the collective discussed the implications of European work (with which I was still unfamiliar) for psychology's premise of the unitary rational subject (Adlam et al., 1977). I also remember how excruciatingly difficult it was to read and understand – a difficulty which I try to address in the following section.

The reasons for my excitement were two-fold. First, soon after graduating with a psychology degree in 1971, I had been employed as a teacher of social psychology in the higher education sector in Britain (this was the epoch of expansion). My dissatisfaction with psychology (social psychology in particular, because that is what I expected most from) became clearer as I tried to teach it in applied settings. It was increasingly difficult to find any redeeming features in it and I wished to find a radically alternative starting point. It was not that I wanted to give up psychological questions – I continued to be fascinated by those.

The second reason for my excitement was that the critique of the unitary rational subject found resonances in my personal experience. Until my mid-20s my life had been sheltered from any real challenges to my sense of my self. My adolescent and student years were untraumatic. On graduating (in 1971), I married the man I had been living with as a student (there was a rash of marriages among that group of so-called anti-establishment students). Then, after a few years, a romantic affair and my increasing sense of an independent self through my job, I came to question seriously my 'choice' of marriage (it felt like something I had just gone along with – but that begs many questions). The decision to leave my marriage, the difficulty of leading a life on my own for the first time, the confusion of my feelings in other relationships with men, and the beginning of my involvement in the women's movement which enabled me to relate intimately with women for the first time in my adult life, all precipitated questions about myself which I felt to be of crucial importance.

At the beginning the questions were something like these: Upon what was my heterosexuality based? Why was I desirous of re-establishing a couple relationship with a man at the same time as being critical of what heterosexual relationships provided in comparison with relationships with women? How was it that I felt more equal to (the same as) the men with whom I had relationships than the women, yet with men felt comfortable in my womanly identity and with women, uncomfortable? The questions revolved around my own identity as a woman – questions which only arose in the course of some major changes as I attempted to discover what independence from a heterosexual relationship might entail.

In the women's movement such questions were widely shared. 'The personal is political' became a slogan which redefined political struggle, turning it into an activity which accompanied every woman participant like a shadow because it involved transforming her relationships with men, women and children – particularly men. The movement opened our eyes to the ways in which we were oppressed by men, and so the fact that most of us lived with them and loved them demanded a whole new definition of politics.

Women were beginning to experience resistance in ourselves to becoming the kind of women that feminist politics wanted us to be. In order to understand that resistance, we not only needed a whole new language and theory, but a method which uncovered an oppression which was multiply camouflaged: unconscious (for example, were we attached to having someone more powerful than ourselves?); taboo (for example, our experience of sex and maybe of violence); private (should you talk to others about the problems in your relationship or is it disloyal?); and taken for granted (of course we did not expect them to shop on their way home from work, but we did). Consciousness-raising, for me, meant much more than a group I went to once a week – it pervaded my entire way of relating to other people. This was strengthened by other aspects of my life.

Since 1973 I had been teaching the social psychology of groups through leading experiential groups. I had started trying out experiential groups (T-groups, encounter groups) soon after graduating. Although I became quite critical of their assumptions about human nature, I can now see the influence that the humanistic climate had, particularly when it came to explaining change. Consequently, I feel that I am in a good position to identify what I believe to be its widespread influences in psychology. (I take humanistic and human relations psychology to be synonymous.) I spent three years (1975–8) as a researcher in a team which used the approach of the

Tavistock Institute of Human Relations (a psychoanalytically based method of action research in groups and organizations) and part of our method as a team was to use the evidence of our own feelings to understand the dynamics we were working with (this daily use of Kleinian theory stood me in good stead later).

Despite this background, and despite doing my Ph.D. when I was already employed in a secure university teaching job in psychology, I still had difficulty in arriving at the point where I could start research with questions about my own self and use consciousness-raising to provide some important principles on which the method could be based. It is because the orthodox methodological principles of psychology are still so powerful and dominant that I want to give an account of how I came to do what I did. The conditions of the 1970s are history, but they have left their legacy, and I know that my research is highly relevant for psychologists (particularly psychology students) in the climate of the late 1980s.[1] For example, Amina Mama, whose Ph.D. I supervised, uses many of the principles of my method and theory to research the identity of black British women, and developed my work in a quite new direction as a result.

I hope that the present book will give psychologists some ideas for proceeding differently with their research and the support and confidence to do so. I am not addressing this hope exclusively to women psychologists, although it was primarily through a women's political culture that I came to develop the approach I did. What I am arguing ties in with the dissatisfactions coming from many spheres, and could be taken up by any psychologist. However, because of the history of psychology and its effects, I see it as being of most immediate relevance in research by and for categories of people marginalized by orthodox Western psychology; women, black and Third World people, working-class people. Amina Mama argues this point as follows:

> Incredibly, traditionalists have argued that research by members of oppressed groups on their own people will somehow be more 'biased' than research by Westerners. At the same time there has also been a Western tradition of studying 'other' groups, invariably groups that are less powerful . . . This in itself is a dynamic that reproduces the power relations prevailing in the social realm. Studies of deviants, abnormals, freaks, obscure cults and subcultures, mentally ill people, women, 'negroes' all need to be viewed in this light. (1987, pp. 169–70)

1

Myself and my Method: from Separation to Relation

The Golden Notebook

At what point can I say that I started doing *research*, as opposed to something which many other women were doing at the time? I was reading widely any feminist literature: history, social anthropology, political economy, language and psychoanalysis; anything on sexuality, homosexuality and sexual identity, and any social theory which seemed to address the problem of the relation between individual and social. I was also living the problem and – again like many women – keeping a journal. Quite early on, my notes became such a mess that I bought a loose-leaf binder, and divided it into sections. I called it my 'Golden Notebook' (the reference being to Doris Lessing's book of that name). Very soon the sections disappeared. Given what I have described, you can imagine that it was impossible to separate 'me' from 'theoretical ideas' from 'field notes'.

I gave up making notes separately on index cards while I was reading, because an idea from a quotation would spark off an idea about the significance of something I had experienced, and the note would develop into an analysis of that experience. I had endless talks with friends, both women and men, and would write notes on these afterwards if it was relevant (it usually was when people were talking about themselves and their relationships). I called these my field notes. For example, after one conversation, dated 25 November 1980, I wrote:

> George and I were talking about being in couples. He went through all the reasons why he'd decided it was best to split up with Charlotte – best for them both. I said I remembered half a dozen times us talking in the past and him concluding that he really should make the break. He agreed. He said, 'I knew I should, I knew I had to, but I couldn't'. In retrospect he could see clearly that he had become dependent upon the relationship and that at the time he'd found all sorts of rationalizations, for example giving it time, Charlotte agreeing (again) to work on it, it upsetting her too much.

Not having kept a journal for years, this now seems to have been an exaggerated preoccupation in my life. Then it seemed important, to me and to those around me (for example, a friend offered me her own journal to use for my research). In retrospect, I feel critical of my insistence on analysing everything in my life during the last year or so of thesis work, when I was involved in a heterosexual relationship which was going wrong. When I was with my partner, every action seemed imbued with so much significance (no doubt it was at some level), that I always had pencil and paper at the ready. Long trains of analysis would be set off by a single comment. There was no distinction between working on the relationship and analysing the reproduction of gender difference in it. In fact it was a very creative period for developing my analysis further. At the same time, however, I was using my ability to analyse what was going on between us to provide me with power to explain away the ambivalence my partner was feeling about the relationship. A feminist discourse (which is one way of describing my position) provided me with knowledge and power to define what was acceptable and un-acceptable between us. It did not alter his ambivalence. (I discuss Foucault's knowledge–power analysis in some detail in Chapter 4.)

The Data

The kind of opportunistic collection of accounts that I describe here was fascinating, and undoubtedly important to my understanding, but I could hardly avoid feeling that it was not psychological research. I therefore resolved to collect some proper data. My first attempt was rather half-hearted. I went to a meeting which had gathered to organize a women's conference on bisexuality. It began with every-one in turn saying why the issue was important to them. It was one of those magical occasions when even a large group of unfamiliar women, interrupted by late arrivals, produced an atmosphere in which deeply personal, insightful and courageous things could be said and respected. I decided to ask to record sessions at the proposed conference. I also used what I had learned from the planning group to construct an open-ended questionnaire on the subject which I left for women at the conference to pick up. I got two replies. Even though these were quite full, it was enough to convince me that this was not the kind of data I was interested in.

I abandoned my attempt to use a 'proper' social-psychological method of data collection and soon after resolved to tape discussions as a way of gathering data (I thought of them as interviews for a long time). I felt ambivalent about this decision because unstructured interviewing did not seem a very acceptable method 7 years ago and I was anxious that talking to people with a tape-recorder would not be acceptable for Ph.D. research in psychology. When I came to des-cribe my methods for the thesis, I called all the sorts of things described above as the exploratory phase, the sort of phrase, like field notes, which gives a tidier impression of what I did than it felt at the time and locates it within the discourse of research.

In my thesis I describe what came next as follows:

> It was during what still felt like part of the exploratory phase, though it was only in retrospect that I would have been able to characterize it thus, that I fixed on the use of consciousness-raising as a central method for generating data, rather than, for example, following up my 'pilot' questionnaire. The decision on method was also a result of the wealth of data, of a unique kind, that I found was coming out of conversations which I could have, either with one person or in a group. In 1979 I 'piloted' this method in the sense that I tried asking one or two people . . . if I could tape record our talks together. The tape recorder did not seem to inhibit such sessions and gradually these developed into the series of nine 'dialogues' from which more than half of the material eventually used in the data analysis chapters is drawn. (Hollway, 1982, p. 214)

This is true, but what it does not record is that it took me until writing up to present what I had done in such a matter-of-fact, non-defensive tone. This was because enjoying myself talking to people who wanted to talk to me did not feel like data gathering. It is only now that I can look at it quite the other way round and say that I succeeded in forging a valuable method: that is, to talk with people in such a manner that they felt able to explore material about themselves and their relationships, past and present, in a searching and insightful way. I did not feel skilful because it came so easily. It was easy because the research participants were people like me and we were continuing an activity that was a vibrant part of our subculture at the time. Now I can believe that this made for good research practice. At the time I was anxious that it was a bit of a con.

What was clear, though, is that the participants wanted to talk – either in the group or to me, or both. This was partly because they were all people who were self-conscious about their lives and relationships and found it useful. It was also because of who I was, that is someone in a similar situation to them, someone who did not withhold my own experience and feelings and someone who not only was happy to listen endlessly, but who asked helpful questions and used an analysis which made sense of their confused experience. In this sense, I became an informal counsellor to quite a few people.

Before I go on to specify who participated in the research and the justification I mounted for choosing them, I mention the other sources of data. Tape-recorded sessions were of three types: the dialogues mentioned above (coded D), the weekend groups (W) and the gender groups (G). (In addition I recorded one women's group (WG) when the opportunity arose.) The weekend groups refer to a residential weekend which I organized when a mixed-sex group of 18 people gathered to explore 'sexuality and relationships' through a consciousness-raising method. Although I advertised the weekend (in *Spare Rib* and *Gay News*), only two were complete strangers. Of

the remainder, I knew ten and six were friends of friends. I com-
mented in my thesis: 'again my inside relationship to a network of
people provided me with contacts which proved more rewarding than
formal methods'.

The gender groups (G) formed, without any prompting from me,
from a subgroup of the weekend group who wanted to continue
meeting for the same purpose. I was invited to be a member and after
the first session it was decided that I could continue tape-recording
the sessions. The transcript on which Chapter 3 is based is taken from
one of these evenings.

I used little of the transcripts from the weekend groups in my
thesis. The reason is that many of the groups examined relationship
processes that were going on at the time. I had invited a friend to help
facilitate the sessions, a man with whom I had worked a lot as a group
process consultant. We had planned how to work at the process level
and I anticipated using a process analysis in my research. In the end,
my analysis moved increasingly away from a group process analysis
(in which by this time I was very experienced) and towards an analysis
which enabled me to theorize the relation between content and
process: gender difference and meaning on the one hand and power
and defence mechanisms on the other (see Chapter 5). A draft
chapter on 'masculine and feminine styles in social relations' got
thrown out of the thesis. In the end I would easily have had enough of
the right kind of material, that is participants' accounts of themselves
and their relationships, without organizing the weekend (though the
subsequent gender groups were a valuable source of material).

It might still not be clear what I mean by a consciousness-raising
method which, to those who have never been in such a group, must
often seem mysterious. Hartsock summarizes the method of consciousness-raising as follows:

> The practice of small-group consciousness-raising – with its stress on
> examining and understanding experience and on connecting personal
> experience to the structures which define women's lives – is the clearest
> example of the method basic to feminism. Through this practice women
> have learned that it was important to build up their analyses from the
> ground up, beginning with their own experiences. (1979, p. 59)

But maybe this is an idealized definition. I sometimes think that even
those who have participated in a consciousness-raising group must
wonder if what they are doing is really consciousness-raising because
there is such a diversity of practices. Some might not want to dignify
their raps with that title, maybe thinking that what they do is simply
'women's talk' or even gossip. But then gossip should not be de-
meaned when it involves exploring your own and other women's
experience cooperatively, that is, with the capacity to identify.

Consciousness-raising was built on older traditions but had a more explicit political edge. It was about women's oppression and, arising from that, how to change ourselves and our relationships, at home and at work.

The method was appropriate in a number of ways: many of the participants shared my familiarity with it; it focuses on the personal while holding wider historical and political issues in view; it lends itself to the use of psychodynamic theory, particularly to the concept of the unconscious; it was consistent with the political commitments of my research which (in the tradition of critical theorists of the Frankfurt School) was 'tied to an emancipatory interest seeking to free men from . . . domination by forces which they do not understand or control' (Giddens, 1979, p. 57).

Naturalism and Social Science

During the period of gathering material, I was looking for work which mounted a solid critique of orthodox psychological methods. Unfortunately, this was not available in psychology (although collections of writings on new paradigms of research, such as that by Reason and Rowan, performed part of that function by arguing against the dehumanizing effects of scientific psychology). This was another area in which I felt obliged to read outside psychology and I was particularly helped by the work of Giddens on the evolution of sociological method and of Bhaskar on the philosophy of social science.

According to Giddens, the social sciences were shaped above all in an encounter with the spectacular advances of natural science and technology in the late-eighteenth and nineteenth centuries. This led to 'an attempt to bring into being a science of society which would reproduce, in the study of human social life, the same kind of sensational illumination and explanatory power already yielded up by the sciences of nature' (Giddens, 1976, p. 13). (He continued: 'by this token, social science must surely be reckoned a failure'.)

Bhaskar's claim that social science could not legitimately aspire to prediction, but only to explanation, has had a profound effect on my thinking about psychology:

> The objects of social science investigation . . . only manifest themselves in 'open systems'; that is in systems where invariant empirical regularities do not obtain. . . . Practically all theories of orthodox philosophy of science, and the methodological directives they secrete, presuppose closed systems. Because of this they are totally inapplicable to the social sciences – which is not of course to say that the attempt cannot be made to apply them – with disastrous consequences. (1978, p. 19)

As a result of the characteristics of open systems, Bhaskar argues, 'the criteria for the rational confirmation and rejection of theories in social science *cannot be predictive* and so must be *exclusively explanatory*' (1978, p. 21). This does not rule out empirical testing: 'once a hypothesis of a causal mechanism has been produced in social science, it can then be tested quite *empirically*, though exclusively by reference to its explanatory power' (1978, p. 21). It was on these principles that I believed the methods of my thesis should be judged.

Bhaskar's critique of naturalism made it possible for me to find a position outside them, rather than just feel an ill-defined disgust with orthodox methods. Bhaskar defines naturalism as the claim that:

> There is an essential unity of method between the natural and social sciences. Its tenets are two: reductionism refers to the position that there is an actual identity of subject matter; scientism refers to the position which denies any significant difference in the methods appropriate to studying social and natural objects. (1979, p. 1)

In effect this means that in the last 100 years naturalism 'has seen science as consisting essentially in the registration of (or refutation of claims about) empirical invariances between discrete events, states of affairs and the like' (1979, p. 21). While it is increasingly being recognized among psychologists that the collection of facts will not add up to produce knowledge, the canons of scientific orthodoxy still dictate what is accepted in mainstream journals and what most examiners will find acceptable in research.

The Separation of Theory and Method
The naturalist tradition has been strongly defended in psychology and has led to an obsession with scientific method. According to Levy (1981), where method has come into conflict with questions it has wanted to ask, it has changed the questions and not the methods. I went about it the other way round. What I had to counteract was the distinction between theory and method which 'is one of the more curious features of social science' (Silverman, 1972, p. 183). The division is encapsulated in the principle of the hypothetico-deductive method which requires that a hypothesis is formulated on the basis of theory and then, quite independently, data is collected which will test this hypothesis. As Silverman points out: 'this rhetoric of verification notably fails to specify how theory is to be generated – except by abstract contemplation' (1972, p. 187). As a result:

> Methodology has come to mean little more than precise statistical techniques for handling quantitative data while 'grand theory' seems more suitable for the arm-chair than the research process. (1972, p. 183)

The grounded theory approach (Glaser and Strauss, 1967) reunites theory and method:

> The concepts that are developed through research, along with the emerging theory, provide guidelines for further collection of data, which further refines the concepts and develops the theory. This further collection is directed by the emerging theory. (Lauer and Handel, 1977, p. 4)

Although I had already begun to do this, discovering grounded theory gave me confidence to continue, and also the terms and legitimacy to represent it in the justification of my methodology.

Statistical and Theoretical Sampling

The consequences of rejecting the objective of prediction and control as the goal of social science are so massive for its methodology that it is difficult to grasp them (I return to this issue in Chapter 6). Here I want to discuss one methodological consequence which was fundamental to my research – abandoning statistical sampling. Experimental and psychometric psychology have in common the use of measurement and, consequently, the dependence upon statistical principles for deriving samples. A sample refers to the selection of people who will be representative of a wider population and thus permit the testing of a hypothesis and its generalization. The concern for mass generalization and the requirement to use large numbers for statistical manipulation together produce knowlege which does not address the complex conditions of people and their conduct, either in their uniqueness or their commonality.

Social anthropology is based on learning information about the generality of a culture through the specificity of different people's accounts. Its method is based on understanding similarities and differences, which is the principle on which theoretical sampling is based (Atkinson, 1977, p. 15). Referring to social anthropological method enabled me to adhere to my belief that whatever anyone said was potentially meaningful, and also enabled me to clarify and formalize the method through the notion of similarities and differences.

By the time I wrote my methodology chapter, I could specify that:

> My basic contention is that a social theory of the subject implies that the information derived from *any participant* is valid because that account is a product (albeit complex) of the social domain. If this domain is analysed in its specificity, the resultant interpretation will be valid without the support of statistical samples; that is, without evidence that whole groups do the same thing. (Hollway, 1982, p. 183)

This principle supported me in the number of participants I found, the criteria for choosing them and eventually in not feeling constrained to include all participants in the analysis, a principle which is relevant only within the paradigm of statistical sampling.

Choosing Participants

I have already described the features of the subculture that influenced my own self-questioning and the formulation of my research. The other participants were people like me in relevant respects: they were of a similar age (around 30 in 1980), class status (though not class background), educational and professional position and, therefore, cultural history. They were not all white. From a wide network of friends, it was easy for me to establish a sense of who would be an appropriate participant. Of course this did not constitute a sample in the statistical sense, and I am sure that the issues I was working with are to some extent particular to a limited group of people. Generalizability is not automatic in this method and has to be established according to theoretical rather than statistical principles.

I identified participants intuitively and formalized my reasons later, using what I found in sociological and social anthropological method to support and legitimate my decisions. I have a horror of using that word 'intuitive', because its associations with women's ways are so derogatory. As I wrote this I was about to find another word until I paused to ask myself why I was censoring it. It is worth exploring therefore what I think my intuitions were based on. My intuition was not some primitive product of my feelings, in contrast to the use of reason (the significance it has through being associated with women). I knew which people were capable of exploring themselves in the kind of way that would tell me something, and I also knew how to relate to them in order to facilitate this. I knew that people with problems or difficulties in their relationships, or people who were living in unorthodox ways with partners, would be more likely to be aware of the issues that I was interested in. It is easy enough to see how people can take their situation for granted if it is 'normal' and therefore have relatively little to say – my own history made me realize it.

When I came to formalize the criteria on which my choice of participants rested, I used the principle of 'sampling according to similarities and differences' from the comparative method:

> I chose the similarities on the basis of the material and discursive criteria outlined above: my participants were all similar to the extent that they did not live the discursive practices of the heterosexual couple without contradictions. In this sense they all had access to the problem area that I predicted would be of crucial importance to the reproduction and change

of gender. Their relation to this unit differed considerably. The dimensions of difference that I outlined before deciding on participants for the weekend group were as follows: single/coupled; lesbian/homosexual/bisexual/heterosexual; celibate/monogamous/having several sexual relations; living with partner/living apart; married/unmarried/separated. Finally, and most important, although I defined my primary focus as the subjective experience of women's gender, it was clearly vital to include men in the information gathered. This was not simply so that I could include both partners in heterosexual couples. It was the result of a recognition of the importance of difference in constituting gender. . . . The basis of the comparative method, which is an important part of 'grounded theory', is that through being faced with differences, concepts are generated which describe those differences which can then be applied to other phenomena. (1982, p. 204)

Self-analysis

I went on to talk about a crucial practical criterion – choosing participants who would actually provide me with more than a rationalized, seamless and abstracted account of themselves:

> One final criterion affected my choice of participants. Although in principle, any account can form the basis of an analysis, in practice there are significant differences in the richness of the accounts of people. To the extent that this derives from the contradictions generated by their circumstances, I have already accounted for it. However, different people do not understand their actions, relations and subjective experience either in the same ways, or to the same extent. The data afforded by someone who 'rationalizes' events is far poorer for my purpose than someone who both experiences and expresses a multiplicity of meanings in their subjective experience. For this reason, where possible I chose participants who practised what I shall generically call 'self analysis' [I include a table of participants with the type of self analysis]. Many different types of experience fit into this criterion: people in psychoanalysis or other kinds of therapy; people doing co-counselling, group work or encounter; people with experience of consciousness-raising – in a men's group or a women's group. In this category I also include people who simply felt it to be a priority to work out the relation of their feelings and actions and situations and who consequently either wrote a journal, or talked openly about such things to friends. This last category is particularly common amongst women who have had some contact with the women's movement, where sharing experiences which are commonly taboo has been a part of the deprivatization of women's experience. The data speaks for itself in this respect, being unusual in the openness and insight with which people treat their experiences. (1982, p. 205)

This can illustrate the circular relation between method and theory, that is, how method has an effect on the production of knowledge and vice versa. Because participants gave me complex, dynamic, multiple and contradictory accounts of themselves and their experience, it was

possible to develop a theory of multiple and contradictory subjectivity. Certain methods would have precluded such material and
hence also precluded the use of such concepts. On the other hand,
because I was developing a critique of the unitary individual subject
of psychology, I sought participants and developed methods which
would be adequate to the theoretical framework.

The Conventions of Scientific Research
I then gave a table of the 33 research participants (under their
pseudonyms) detailing domestic situation, sexuality, age, occupation
and type of self-analysis and other tables which provided breakdowns
of numbers within these headings. I calculated how many hours of
tapes I had in each category (D,W and G) – just under 60 hours
altogether – translated it into units of text and tabulated what
proportion of each category I had used in the final analysis. I also
tabulated the people by the events they had participated in and the
number of times they appeared in the final text. Tabulating information was a sensible way of summarizing disparate information, but
my limited attempt was also driven by anxieties about proper psychological method.

Since there existed no protocols in psychological research for
dealing with the relative lack of structure and the open-endedness of
consciousness-raising, followed by interpretative analysis, I had no
guide for how much data I should collect, from how many people and
how I should transcribe it. I worried about using too few people (with
the principles of statistical sampling lurking) and yet I ended up with
far too much data. I concluded a section on 'the problem of too much
data' by saying 'I could have limited my initial data gathering to a half
or quarter of my sixty hours and had what I needed to give evidence
for my theoretical assertions' (1982, p. 248).

Verstehen and Ethnomethodology
There are traditions in social science research which have developed
ways of interpreting unstructured data derived from uncontrolled
social settings and I turned to these for a theoretical rationale of my
method.

The major contending epistemology to naturalism in the social
sciences has been the hermeneutic tradition which centres on the
concept of Verstehen (understanding). In contrast to naturalism's
treatment of people like any other object of study, Verstehen is based
on the assertion of two basic differences between the study of natural
and social objects: the latter are characterized by agency and
meaning. One of Verstehen's claims is important for methodology:
the social sciences deal with a preinterpreted reality and 'anyone who

recognizes that self-reflection, as mediated linguistically, is integral to the characterization of human social conduct, must acknowledge that such holds also for his own activities as a social "analyst"' (Giddens, 1976, preface). Consequently, 'the concepts employed by the social scientist are linked to (or depend on a prior understanding of), those used by laymen in sustaining a meaningful social world' (1976, p. 52).

Ethnomethodology is 'the study of ordinary people's methods of producing and making sense of everyday life' (Potter and Wetherell, 1987, p. 18). As is evident from this definition, it derives from the Verstehen tradition. It shares the weaknesses of Verstehen which boil down to the criticism that it is idealist (see Bhaskar, 1979, p. 22ff., for a detailed critique). Ethnomethodology's concept of 'natural language' depends on the assumption that the text speaks for itself and argues that it does so on the basis of shared meanings between speaker/writer, researcher and reader. It claims that 'sense and reference can be settled by looking at features of their context or occasions of use' (Potter and Wetherell, 1987, p. 23) and that ordinary people are constantly engaged in this interpretative work. This assumes a unitary society which spawns common meanings. As a result, the model works well enough to explain the success of communication, but it camouflages the enormous variability of meanings and gives no analytical leverage on what Lacan called 'the success of miscommunication'.

A common criticism of ethnomethodology has been that it relies on unexplicated commonsense assumptions itself (Potter and Wetherell, 1987, p. 30). However, rather than develop a theory of meaning which raises questions about 'natural language', many ethnomethodologists' response to this criticism has been to 'adopt a new analytic strategy known as conversation analysis based primarily on verbatim transcripts of interaction rather than on field notes or the researcher's remembered experiences' (1987, p. 30). In trying to find fact where only the multiplicity and volatility of meaning reside, conversation analysts are conceding to positivist assumptions about the reliability and validity of research data. The response demonstrates how, for lack of an adequate theory of meaning, ethnomethodology has been caught between two philosophical traditions in social science – the naturalist and the Verstehen traditions.

Transcribing and Coding
This left me without any ready-made methods of data analysis, from either inside or outside psychology. Did I have to transcribe all that was recorded? Psychological method told me that I should because

otherwise my selections would be arbitrary. In the thesis I pointed out that because I had not used a structured and limiting format, much of the material did not correspond with the focus of my research concern. To justify this I had to look behind the pre-scriptions of psychological method and remind myself that I was not imposing formal boundaries around research situations like an ex-periment, or even like an interview conducted according to a schedule. Content analysis (the most similar method to discourse analysis that psychology has) establishes such boundaries around what it defines as data and then requires that everything be trans-cribed because all instances of a word or phrase must be used (see Potter and Wetherell, 1987). But content analysis is based on assumptions about quantities of things.

When I considered the principles of content analysis in the light of what I had actually done, they were inappropriate. For example, in my dialogue with Martha, I had gone round with my tape-recorder and she had cooked supper. We were well into the discussion by the time it was ready (sounds on the tape of casserole dishes being put down and wine being poured into glasses) and we just left the tape-recorder on throughout the meal. Her partner Martin, who was an old friend of mine, arrived back unexpectedly during the meal. Martha summarized what we had been talking about (in which he was central) and his comments were therefore recorded. They turned out to be particularly valuable in helping me to make a conceptual link between power, need and misrecognition (see Hollway, 1984 a and b). But, I reasoned, if the boundary between the tape-recorder being on or off is so arbitrary in terms of what people say, why should I fetishize everything that was on it?

Faced with 60 hours of tape-recorded material, I went through the tapes and made thorough summaries of the content. I did this as soon as possible after the session, not only so that it was fresh in my memory, but because it was useful to integrate my analysis into future discussion. Then I went through the summaries marking the chunks that I reckoned were interesting and relevant (a judgement based on all the experience and theoretical work to that point). Then I transcribed the marked parts. At one point I employed a transcriber, but she was unable to make sense of it like I could. I recognized the extent to which I was an insider in the network of participants, and how much understanding I retained from my presence at the time of most recordings.

Transcribing procedures posed a similar set of problems. The quest for a perfectly accurate transcript reflects the dictate of empiricism that data provide the foundation for proof. Driven by such a search, linguistic analysis has tried to pin down meaning beyond words by incorporating conventions for transcribing microscopic extra-linguistic features such as the length of pauses. At the beginning I evolved a procedure for transcribing such aspects because it was consistent with my interest in process. But the detailed adherence to such a procedure makes the text virtually unreadable, and I realized that it was rarely contributing to my analysis, which was shifting from process to content as I began to use a Foucauldian discourse analysis.

Making sense of the transcript in terms of the research questions is the most harrowing part of all. The more unstructured it is, the greater the anxiety that it is going to be impossible to analyse rigorously. I tried coding the transcripts according to the themes I was identifying as important (these changed over time as my theoretical framework developed). Assuming that I would use all occurrences, I marked all instances of a word or idea (for example, 'mentors' or 'jealousy'). I developed a code (which I rejected later) which had six major theoretical categories (history, signification, social relations, identity/subjectivity, difference, discourses). Under these were subheadings (changing subjectivity, power, need) and then sub-subheadings (jealousy, dependence, threat/defence/repression, fantasy). I arranged all the data according to these and cut and pasted in order to reorganize it into the categories. I concluded:

> The result was unsatisfactory in several respects. Most importantly, it made me realize that what I was trying to understand was a complex whole, and the categories were only of explanatory status. By separating them, I was doing violence to the relations between categories, which were internal relations in a whole. I lost the integrity of a case-study of a person or couple which could illustrate the relations between these aspects. In fact the relations *between* categories were far more important than the coding of a piece of transcript according to one or several categories: if I could not demonstrate the relations, my analysis would indeed be useless. The relations were best demonstrated by the integrity of someone's experience, or the way a group explored a particular theme. I realized that these shouldn't be chopped up in the interest of methodological 'rigour' which was more characteristic of naturalism. (1982, p. 257)

All of these transgressions in terms of orthodox psychological method understandably made me anxious. What was important at the time was that I risked following the dictates of my own reasoning and postponed, until the write-up of the methodology chapter, a thorough and formal justification of them: my methodology chapter was 100 pages long as a result. The following section covers some of the theoretical issues it dealt with.

Democracy and Power Relations

The principles of Verstehen have contributed to a democratic tradition in social science research which stipulates that the researcher should not presume to know more about what the participant means (maybe should presume to know less, because the participant is a bona fide member of the culture being researched). The researcher's resources are the same as those of 'lay actors': stocks of knowledge and meaning frames.

Where naturalism dealt with power relations through erecting the notion of objectivity, the interpretative sociologies camouflaged them by superimposing democracy. (I return to this issue in my discussion of feminist social psychology in Chapter 3). In Foucault's theory, the knowledge/power relation is applied above all to the production of the human sciences. It implies that researchers, through their position as experts, will have considerable power. According to Foucault, power is present and productive in all social relations and the relations of research are no exception. I argued that this cannot be dealt with by being silent in the research situation because lack of information only leaves the field open for participants' assumptions to affect their relation to the research – assumptions which may or may not be misleading. In the thesis I stated that:

> My commitment to participating in the research thus derives not only from the recognition that I am as appropriate a participant as any, but also that it is consistent with my analysis of the relations of research. By taking the same kinds of risks of disclosure and exploration as other people my position as researcher is more likely to be demystified. Similarly, by interpreting what I understand to be happening, or giving my understanding of somebody's account, or comparing their experience with my own, the power of my 'theory' as opposed to anyone else's is likely to be reduced. I do not draw the positivist distinction between the 'theory' of the scientist as opposed to the ignorance of the 'subject'. However neither do I share the ethnomethodologists' counter-position.
>
> The self-analysis that my participants have engaged in, their sharing of experiences and reading, cannot be reduced to an unproblematized category of 'natural language' or 'common sense' which distinguishes no difference between people's understandings. (1982, p. 235)

I went on to point out that because of whom I had chosen to participate, the differences between me and them were much reduced and, as can be seen from the transcripts, I was by no means the only one to interpret or challenge people's accounts.

Much new paradigm research has taken on the concern for democracy (as has feminist psychology, see Chapter 6) by involving participants in the analysis and by asking what effects the research has had on participants. This is sometimes used as the criterion of whether research is emancipatory. In my thesis (1982, pp. 273–9) I go into detail about how I showed relevant extracts to participants and how I treated their replies. As regards the effects of the research process on participants, it is difficult to be specific. The sessions were part of a process of self-exploration in which all participants, to a greater or lesser extent, were engaged and there is no way to separate out the parts.

In this book my emphasis is not on the participants' relation to the research. I want rather to stress that the production of knowledge has wider political effects than on the participants and researcher. The direction of the book is to broaden the scope to look at the production of psychological knowledges and to understand how subjectivity and power relations are implicated in this process, in particular the results of gender difference. I want this book to provide an example of an alternative theory of subjectivity and an alternative method for psychology. In my theory, this is bound to include a different relation of the researcher to participants, but it also involves a different relation of the researcher to knowledge. This point is developed further in Chapter 7.

2

'isms' and 'ivity': a Guide to Basic Terminology and its Allegiances

Terminology and Jargon

From this point onwards in the book, I begin to use terminology which is unfamilar to most psychologists. This terminology becomes necessary when, instead of concentrating on a critique as in the previous chapter, I start to use alternative theories in analysing participants' accounts. All the terms are relevant to understanding how meaning and subjectivity can be theorized. In this chapter, I summarize the debates within which these new concepts have emerged, and locate them in relation to outstanding theoretical questions.

I do not expect that the following explanation of terms and their theoretical context will make much more than abstract sense at this stage. Those of you who become irritated by the unfamiliarity of the terminology, I ask to hang on. New concepts really only become understandable, not through terse definition, but through continued use and exemplification. Many of these concepts – for example, positions in discourses – crop up time and again in the context of a detailed analysis of my research material, and thereby become familiar and their powerful explanatory value understood. My response to the charge of difficult terminology is often not to modify the concepts but to try to avoid using them in the abstract.

The main problem of terminology in theory construction is a simple contradiction: if you use old terminology, it will govern your thinking in the same direction, because it holds that old set of theoretical assumptions. If you use new terminology or, to be more accurate, terminology developed to be adequate to the new ways of thinking, readers who have been schooled in an opposing tradition (as psychologists have) will get irritated because they cannot understand. If they give up, the effort is wasted. We were caught in this contradiction when we wrote *Changing the Subject* (Henriques et al., 1984), whose aim was to apply post-structuralist theory to psychology and in so doing to make an intervention in psychology. Reviews by psychologists invariably criticized the language. At the time post-structuralism was new to Britain and I was discovering as I went along where the concepts could take me. I was new to the whole venture, too mystified by those who seemed to be in the know to criticize their terminology. Now I feel more confident about making the distinction for this book between what is unnecessarily abstruse and what is essential for thinking about people in new ways.

The Subject and Subjectivity

I have come to the conclusion that the term 'subjectivity' cannot be replaced by either 'individual' (the reasons for which should be clear from this entire section), 'self' or 'identity' (the term 'psyche' is useful to refer to the multiple forces governing subjectivity and action). 'Self' is a term which has been at the centre of considerable philosophical and psychological theorization (for example, Mischel, 1977). In my thesis I reviewed this literature and concluded that it was caught up in the problem of dualism between individual and society which the new theories of the subject were trying to overcome. Even shorn of these connotations, it is difficult to use either 'self' or 'identity' without the implication that it consists of what we experience. Since it is an important part of my project to encompass within the analysis what is not directly accessible to experience, I decided not to use either term, despite their familiarity. So subjectivity it is. On a positive note, I have reclaimed what have been the derogatory connotations of subjectivity, as opposed to objectivity (see Chapter 6). My theorizing displaces objective rationality from the centre of the human subject and produces radical possibilities for the use of subjective knowledge.

Subjectivity is the central theoretical concept of this book and can, therefore, only be thoroughly conceptualized by the end of it. Frosh (1987, p. 11) uses the term synonymously with 'ideas, beliefs and emotions', thus trying to refer to the person in ways which are inclusive and also familiar. In *Changing the Subject* I and my co-authors summed up as follows:

> We use 'subjectivity' to refer to individuality and self-awareness – the condition of being a subject – but understand in this usage that subjects are dynamic and multiple, always positioned in relation to discourses and practices and produced by these – the condition of being subject'. (Henriques et al., 1984, p. 3)

This is what subjectivity means for post-structuralism. Its use represents a theoretical development from the notion of the subject in structuralism (see below for an explanation of both these 'isms'):

> The 'subject' is the generic term used in philosophy for what in lay terms would be 'the person', 'the individual' or 'the human being', and what in psychology is referred to as 'the individual'. The term 'theories of the subject' has tended to refer to approaches which are critical of

psychology's assumptions about individuality, theoretical approaches which emphasize the way in which the social domain constitutes the individual, rather than the other way round. (Henriques et al., 1984, p. 2)

In what follows I will summarize the theoretical debates that have brought the term subjectivity into being.

Humanism

The humanism/anti-humanism debate was largely the product of European thinkers and it was not until Althusser that it became familiar to more than a few British social scientists. Typical of the European traditions of grand theory, the debate has been conducted on a fairly abstract and philosophical plane. None the less, it is one with fundamental importance for political action because it concerns the nature of social change (see Henriques et al., 1984, p. 93ff., for a summary of this debate and its implications). The debate, whose origins are within Marxist theory, concerns the status of the human subject in philosophy and social science and the implications of humanist theories for political change:

> The humanist position tends to see the individual as the agent of all social phenomena and productions, including knowledge. The specific notion of the individual contained in this outlook is one of a unitary, essentially non-contradictory and above all rational entity. It is the Cartesian subject in modern form; a notion of the subject which has been central to the whole of western philosophy founded on the principle of the cogito. . . . Taking a stance firmly on the social side of the dualist divide, both structuralism and Marxism have taken as their target this notion of the individual as agent of change. (Henriques et al., 1984, p. 93)

In general, British psychologists, schooled within the positivist scientific tradition and as a result unfamiliar with (and often defensive about) grand theory, were unaware of this debate. But psychology was none the less positioned within it.

Human Relations

By the 1960s, the unitary, rational individual of positivist psychology was no longer the sole voice of psychology and it was from within the human relations alternative that I found a position from which to criticize psychology.[1] Human relations, or humanistic, psychology challenged experimental psychology for not treating the individual as a whole person. However, probably its greatest impact was in the widespread availability of experiential groups whose goal was personal change.

Human relations psychology replaced the rational subject with the feeling subject as the essence of individuality.[2] I remember sitting in endless encounter groups where the best intervention to make was supposedly to ask someone, 'Yes, but what do you *feel*?' If some people had difficulty in getting in touch with their feelings, it was because they were hidden under layers of socialization which could be peeled off in the climate of trust that the human relations group was intent on providing. The idea of a core individual, an essence prior to socialization, is central to this model. Feelings then become products of nature and not of culture; bearers of the truth about the individual. Over the years human relations groups moved away from an analysis of the group or even the interpersonal, to a fascination with what was inside the individual, where, according to human relations, radical change chould take place.

This position is called 'voluntarism' and it is based on the humanist premise that change is initiated by the individual and depends on the individual's choice. On the other side is the position that change (including individual change) is achieved by a change in structures (the orthodox Marxist position). Understanding social change has been dogged by the same dualism as the humanism debate, but when it focuses on this question, the debate goes under the title 'agency –determinism'.

To capture its importance, let me offer a 'parable'. Supposing in one way or another all humanistic psychological intervention was based on the assumption that change was desirable and that the individual is the source of change; that is that change in feelings, perceptions and attitudes resulted in changed action, and that social change consisted of the sum of individual changes (my example of unemployability, below, gives a real instance). Suppose that this assumption were wrong. Its effect would be to preserve the illusion of commitment to change while reproducing the status quo. This would be particularly convincing since those committed to it would be sincere. (Some of you may recognize the critique of liberalism – see Grimshaw, 1986.) To continue the parable, let us suppose these well-intentioned humanist psychologists were criticized by Marxists whose agenda for social change depended on changing basic economic, political and social structures and rejected the notion of personal change. Suppose the humanistic psychologists were under-standably disgusted by the crudeness of this position which failed entirely to address their own experience, and that they were strength-ened in their own beliefs.

Post-structuralism is about trying to transcend this hopeless dualism, by rejecting both voluntarism and determinism. To do so it requires a theory of the subject which is not caught up in the parallel dualism of individual and society.

Individual–Society Dualism
This dualism refers to the way in which social science – and for that matter lay explanations – are based on the assumption of a duality between the individual and the social (see Henriques et al., 1984, Part I, for an extended discussion and critique). For psychology, the social realm is always 'context'; that is, always external to the individual and to some extent artificial. Once the individual and social are assumed to be different things, the problem of their manner of relation is central. Social psychology has depended on the idea of 'interaction':

> Attempts from within psychology to cope with the theoretical problems . . . have tended to resolve themselves into the mere making of statements to the effect that a 'complex interaction' is at work, as if all the problems were solved thereby. (Riley, 1978, p. 79)

According to Riley, the result is an endless uneasy redistribution of balance – which leaves untouched the epistemological problems of the terms and leaves empty the crucial space (1978, p. 74). The crucial space is the person.

The idea of interaction between individual and society underpins social psychology, the subdiscipline whose unenviable responsibility it is to understand the links between individual and social. Social psychology's basic theories depend on this duality: socialization, social cognition, sex-roles and stereotyping. In each case the idea of the subject involved is an individual with an asocial core (it has to be because the social bits are contained in the other half of the dualism). This individual essence rather inevitably reduces to biology and information-processing mechanisms (see Chapter 6 for further discussion).

The Unitary Rational Subject
Psychology's subject then is the individual, and this individual is the transcendental subject of Western philosophy, the one whose essence precedes and is independent of experience or the social realm. The term 'transcendental subject' was used by Kant to refer to the elements of the mind or of consciousness which were not derived from experience. It thus assumes a subject who is equipped to know, and who is the source of ideas. (It is easy to see how this is the subject of mainstream experimental psychology with its exclusive focus on perception, cognition and memory.) The new theories of the subject have been based on a critique of the dominance of this subject in Western thought.

Psychology, in an attempt to distance itself from its philosophical roots, for a long time studiously avoided paying attention to any 'inner entity'. The epitome of this trend was behaviourism, with its avoidance of questions concerning agency and the self. However, behaviourism only avoided the issue and did not unsettle the deep-rooted assumption that the human individual was unitary (that is, that all that characterized *him* came from a single source) and rational (that is, that rationality provides the correct tendency of human thought and action).

The Subject of Psychoanalysis

Freudian theory challenged the unitary rational subject through its core notion of the dynamic unconscious:

> The idea that in each of us there is a realm of psychological functioning which is not accessible to ordinary introspection, but which nevertheless has a determining or at least a motivating influence on the activities, thoughts and emotions of everyday life. (Frosh, 1987, p. 2)

Psychoanalysis provides an explanation for the unconscious:

> The activities of desire, condensed or displayed by the machinations of repression, make sense of the seemingly inexplicable, tell us more about ourselves than we might wish to know. Behaviour is motivated, but the motivations are in some way dangerous and unacceptable, and therefore become hidden. Implicit in this formulation is the notion that the state of reason, of informed and conscious control over one's psychological 'self', is not a state of nature, but of culture – that is, it has to be striven for and constructed. This is one of the sources of the subversive impact of psychoanalysis: it overturns the western view that the distinguishing mark of humanity is reason and rationality. (Frosh, 1987, p. 25)

This quotation makes clear that the Freudian view offers an alternative to the unitary rational subject: it is not that rationality is non-existent, rather that it is always being contested by forces which derive from 'another site'. This is the unconscious, which is the location of repressed material – ideas, feelings, desires and fantasies. Rather than disappearing, this material is constantly threatening to obtrude, and is constantly controlled by the defence mechanisms. It is not just kept down but transformed, through displacement or projection, to appear in other guises or other places. The concept of defence mechanisms plays an important part in my subsequent analysis (see Chapter 5). The forces governing subjectivity and action are therefore not derived from a single source.

Structuralism
Structuralism is the label for any social science approach which conceptualizes social phenomena in terms of structures and, accordingly, prefers to analyse a static slice of life over a dynamic one. It usually asserts the primacy of structures over individual actions in determining the status quo and how change occurs. Most important for present purposes is the revolution that occurred in linguistics on the basis of Saussure's theorization of meaning. What earns Saussure the label structuralist is his 'insistence on a pre-given, fixed structuring of language, prior to its realization in speech or writing' (Weedon, 1987, p. 23). This theorization of language became the foundation of Lacan's structuralist and psychoanalytic account of the subject.

Psychoanalysis has been subject to both humanist and anti-humanist tendencies (Frosh, 1987, gives a very useful account of the different schools of psychoanalysis in these terms). Lacan takes the most structural propositions of Freud's theory (the Oedipal situation and castration complex) and combines them with developments in structuralist linguistics to produce his intransigently anti-humanist account of the emergence of the human subject in infancy: 'he argues for the literal dominance of the "word" over the construction of psychic organization' (Frosh, 1987, p. 131).

Post-structuralism

> All forms of poststructuralism assume that meaning is constituted within language and is not guaranteed by the subject which speaks it. In this sense, all poststructuralism is post-Saussurean. . . . Psychoanalytic forms of poststructuralism look to a fixed psycho-sexual order; deconstruction looks to the relationship between different texts; and Foucauldian theory, which is arguably of most interest to feminists, looks to historically specific discursive relations and social practices. (Weedon, 1987, p. 22)

Foucault's approach provides the principles of an alternative which corrects the static and universalizing tendency of Lacan (see Chapter 5). It gives an account, not of the universal human subject, but of the historical production of specific modern subject forms. The production of knowledge is not neutral, but is the consequence, as well as the condition, of power relations. Foucault symbolizes this reciprocal relation between power and knowledge by writing it as 'power/knowledge'. A contemporary example is how the idea of 'unemployability' gets produced (with the help of psychology, which also legitimizes it) and, alongside power from other sources, helps to produce certain practices:

> Through the concept of unemployability the unemployed can become
> identified (and indeed identify themselves) as a cause of unemployment.
> As a result of such psychologically reinforced explanations, solutions are
> found which perpetuate the status quo: the unemployable can be trained
> in interpersonal skills but the number of jobs does not increase.
> (Henriques et al., 1984, pp. 1–2)

Post-structuralism deconstructs the subject-as-agent and the unitary individual; that is, it provides a critique which gets underneath
what is taken for granted by those terms (see Henriques et al., 1984,
pp. 203–4). However, the emphasis on the production of modern
subject forms within power/knowledge relations does not account for
how a category like unemployable becomes involved in the subjectivity of different unemployed people. Understanding the subject,
in this case the unemployable, as a position in discourse leaves some
problems:

> In this view the subject is composed of, or exists as, a set of multiple and
> contradictory positionings or subjectivities. But how are such fragments
> held together? Are we to assume, as some applications of post-
> structuralism have implied, that the individual subject is simply the sum
> total of all positions in discourses since birth? If this is the case, what
> accounts for the continuity of the subject and the subjective experience of
> identity? What accounts for the predictability of people's actions, as they
> repeatedly position themselves within particular discourses? Can
> people's wishes and desires be encompassed in an account of discursive
> relations? (Henriques et al., 1984, p. 204)

My work attempts to answer these questions within a
post-structuralist framework which integrates psychoanalytic and
Foucauldian emphases. What I think is unique about it is the material
I use. Psychoanalytic post-structuralism has used clinical material;
deconstruction, literary texts; Foucauldian post-structuralism has
taken history as its text. I have helped people to produce accounts
which are relevant to my questions about subjectivity and gender,
and based my theorization on these. To the extent that this book (as
opposed to my thesis) has a methodological focus, it emphasizes what
kind of a theory of subjectivity is necessary to govern how one
extracts meaning from such texts.

3

Meaning and Method

As a result of my reading it was easier to know how not to analyse research accounts than to find an acceptable, consistently theorized way of understanding them. In the earlier stages of trying to make sense of the transcribed material, I was guided by my own strong sense that I knew what was significant in participants' accounts. As I discussed in Chapter 1, this 'intuition' was, of course, a product of concepts and theories that I had assimilated into my own under-standing. Probably the most straightforward way to have formalized and legitimated that knowledge would have been to call it ethnomethodology, which, as I have argued, is based on the principles of Verstehen and asserts the common knowledges between researcher and participants. However, I rejected ethnomethodology for the reasons that I have discussed in Chapter 1. In short, it provides no theory of meaning, nor of its relation to subjectivity.

I was influenced by psychoanalytic concepts, in particular those which could be applied to understanding the dynamics between people, rather than the dynamics within someone's psyche. I refer to these as relational dynamics or processes. My experience in interpreting group process meant that the first things I tended to notice in analysing participants' accounts were these relational dynamics. This was particularly salient when I was analysing material from the weekend and gender groups. However, it also informed my under-standing of the accounts of a person's relationships which s/he gave me in the dialogues. In the first part of this chapter, through the use of a series of extracts from one of the gender groups, I shall try to show what are the strengths and weaknesses of a process analysis and why I needed to develop my particular brand of discourse analysis, which I call interpretative discourse analysis.

Discourse and Social Psychology

Discourse analysis, which unlike the other approaches can provide a theory of meaning, has only recently been taken up seriously as a method for social psychology, notably by Potter and Wetherell (1987) in *Discourse and Social Psychology*. Their starting principle is the primacy of language and text (written or spoken) as the site for investigating social psychological issues. This principle is practically the only thing which the many variants of discourse analysis have in common, for the term has come to cover virtually any approach which analyses text, from cognitive linguistics to deconstruction. My own use of the term 'discourse' is indebted to Foucault, for whom the term is integrated in an analysis of the production of knowledges (or discourses) within power relations. To complicate matters, however, the term 'discourse analysis' is not often used in connection with Foucault's work!

My use of the terms discourse and discourse analysis are illustrated below, where I discuss the extracts. Here I want to make clear one of the ways in which my approach differs both from a Foucauldian analysis and from the use of deconstruction in the analysis of literary texts. My ultimate concern is to apply a theory of the relation between meaning and subjectivity. This necessitates rejecting any version of discourse analysis, such as cognitive linguistics, which starts with the individual. In the context of this chapter's emphasis on method, my aim is to apply interpretative discourse analysis in a way which can be used as a psychological method; that is, a method which incorporates questions about the relation between subjectivity and meaning. In this way I shall have a theoretical guide for the analysis of people's accounts of themselves, their experience and their relations to others.

Potter and Wetherell's book represents the most critical and radical application of discourse analysis to social psychology yet produced. In their view: 'One of the primary goals of discourse analysis is to clarify the linguistic resources used to make certain things happen' (1987, p. 171). This formulation represents an attempt to get away from idealist views of language by not featuring the individual at its centre. Consistent with non-idealist approaches to language, they emphasize discourse as a construction and not as the description of preformed ideas (1987, p. 33). However, in order to achieve this, they explicitly bypass a psychological theory and its relation to language. For example, in addressing the question 'Why did these people do that?' they argue:

> The researcher should bracket off the whole issue of the quality of accounts as accurate or inaccurate descriptions of mental states . . . Our focus is exclusively on discourse itself: how it is constructed, its functions and the consequences which arise from different discursive organization. (1987, p. 178)

While I agree with the desirability of an approach to discourse which is not dictated by the question of truth and falsity, I believe it would be a mistake to throw out the baby of subjectivity with the bathwater of accuracy. That is why I would like to contribute an underlying theory for discourse analysis which is able to understand the relation between meaning and subjectivity.

In the following section I take an extract from one of the gender groups in which Will has difficulty in making an announcement. I discuss its interpretation from a process perspective and use the idea of Will's position in a discourse concerning marriage as the basis for incorporating psychological questions into a discourse analysis. Following that, I consider the implications for feminist psychological methodology and its limitations.

'It's amusing – I mean it's terrible really'

[*George has been encouraging Will to say more about something he hinted at last week.*]

Will: Well, not really, I suppose, it's 'cos[. . .] it changes very much, what I want to talk about. I mean, I know there are lots of things, um [*sighs*] – I mean there are things – you know there are lots of things – um – I feel, in one way quite – I respond to what Malcolm said about thinking that some things about my life are quite sorted out, and I don't need, you know, I'm not in a period of major structural crisis, in a way, but there are lots of problems even – about the things I have sorted out. You know. At another level I actually quite dislike in myself the complacency that I have when I say, well I'm quite happy, I'm doing the sort of work I like doing which is teaching and at the moment I'm having the kind of relationship with Beverley which I quite like and um [. . .] not 'quite like' – that's a bit – I mean that's interesting you see 'cos I say that, whereas actually as it were, this week umm, you know it's been an absolutely extraordinary week for me because um [. . .] Beverley and I have decided to get *married*, right [*noises of response from others*] whereas what I say [*Janice amused, laughing*] is my relationship with Beverley is getting along quite well, it's amusing [*laughs shortly*] – I mean it's terrible actually. That's what [*stutters*], that's one of the things that happened this week among others. The other is that an hour ago a woman with whom I had a relationship until January rang up and I had to say [. . .] I had to tell her about Beverley and she slammed the phone down and I feel quite wobbly about that, and what I say is 'Well [*puts on a voice*] things in my life are going quite well.' [*Janice laughs friendlily*] And I think that is actually – I don't know whether it is to do with sexism but certainly it is to do with a level of abstraction about myself that I get into terribly easily [*Norman: Mmm*] and occasionally pick myself up on like just then and occasionally hardly notice that I'm doing it umm [. . .] and that's a real problem, actually I mean. And with Beverley I don't do it, and with people I know well I don't do umm and I would like to know, I have some idea why I'm doing it [*Norman: Mmm*] in this particular group and in the larger group [*big sigh*], but anyway that's one thing I would like – in some way, for that type of problem to be worked on, because it's the thing I slip into easily and it makes me scream, and very often I come away from groups saying 'as usual I said nothing about myself' [*Janice and Norman laugh*] you know, as usual – or I said it in that way, you know, 'getting on quite well' – 'had an interesting week –

what are your problems George?' [*parodying*] (E3.1, G2.14: Will, George, Janice, Norman, Nicholas and Malcolm)

In this extract, Will is working up to something which he might never have said. There are two features which signal the announcement, but we only know what they are leading to in retrospect. The first is that Will has something on his mind and he is signalling this indirectly by his emphatic repetition of 'There are lots of things (I could say)'. The second is that after the long-winded build up, he says something the effect of which is to show himself in the opposite light from what has happened in the week. His claim, 'I'm not in a period of major structural crisis' in fact signals its opposite and he feels the need to rehearse the stability of other aspects of his life, notably his job. These points could be part of a process analysis which focused on the relation between those present and the speaker and its effects on what is said and unsaid.

From a social-psychological process perspective, it is obvious that Will is inhibited in the group from saying something 'on his mind'. The obstacles are located in the interpersonal or group process and the implication is that *he* is inhibited and can be encouraged (in a human relations paradigm, by trust-building). Will's own account of why he talks at such a level of abstraction combines these two explanations, one about the inhibiting group process, the other about his personality, or his own hang-ups, possibly relating to his masculinity. The former is consistent with a social-psychological process analysis, and the latter a human-relations process analysis. This is not surprising: Will has been to a great many human relations-type groups and treats the gender group as one (part of his problem in the group is that Malcolm, in particular, does not share this discourse and practice).

A process analysis assumes that inside Will there exist ideas already formed. The problem, for process analysis, is defined as the personal and interpersonal conditions which will either facilitate or inhibit their expression. The advantage of such an analysis is that it does raise questions about Will's relation to the others: why are there obstacles to saying that he and Beverley are going to get married? Following up those questions can invoke concepts such as anxiety and repression which call into question simple notions of natural language. Therefore, it does enable some concepts concerning sub-jectivity.

However, this argument depends on the idea that there is a stock of things ready to be said. In a research setting it is assumed that the researcher requires only skill and neutrality in order to get them to be spoken in a truthful manner. For example, accounts from Will could be combed in order to assess the truthfulness of Will's claim that

'With Beverley I don't do it, and with people I know well I don't umm . . .' His claim expresses what he hopes to be the case ('It's one of the reasons I value my relationship with Beverley'). The way he tails off in the middle of making this claim indicates that he recognizes that it is not strictly true even before he finishes the sentence. (For this kind of analysis, transcribing pauses and other non-verbal signals is necessary.) The question about truth or falsity assumes that there is an experience which he has, that words then represent. This premise is based in idealism. In my view the things Will could have said were, in an important sense, inexhaustible. Potter and Wetherell mount a similar criticism in arguing that social psychology has suppressed the variability that it finds in accounts and, by talking in terms of bias and distortion, assumes 'a realm where some descriptions will simply and neutrally reflect reality' (1987, p. 86).

Putting the Text to Work

My analysis depends on rejecting the assumption that I necessarily use the same discourses as my participants. In the case of my analysis of the above extract for my thesis, I did, initially, use a process approach. In what follows, I do not. My choice is based on a clearer recognition of what analytical work I want to do through using the extract. Any extract is chosen for a purpose. In that sense its significance is not a property of the extract, but of the work it is put to do. I have shown how the interpretation could have followed the theory of the participant, had I not other questions in mind, developed during prior analysis and related to my theoretical position. Through having formulated a different question, I found meaning in different parts of the transcribed discussion. Had Will and others never got around to having that discussion – which could easily have happened – I presume I would have used an extract from somewhere else in the transcripts. If I had been present, as a researcher already equipped with the theoretical perspective that I am using now, I could have asked the questions relevant to my theoretical interests and in this way helped to produce material which was appropriate to them. In other words, text is produced – in this case for research. It is not the expression of immanent ideas awaiting expression.

The Meaning of Marriage

The following extract (E3.2) indicates that there are a multiplicity of discourses concerning marriage being expressed in the group and these are being negotiated, not only to establish common sense, but because they have implications for power and the evaluation of people's actions. Therefore, an alternative way of looking at this extract is to ask what discourse Will is expressing and how this reflects upon his conduct and self-evaluation. I can now re-pose the process question with a different emphasis: Why is it difficult to announce the decision to get married? What does getting married mean to Will and Beverley and what does Will think it means to the others present?

Conventionally, marriage is meant to be an announcement of great happiness. Janice responds in such a manner when, later, she says 'Congratulations' and 'Why aren't you effervescing?', but this is not the dominant discourse expressed in people's comments. After Will's announcement, the discussion does not return to marriage for over 5 minutes, during which time an abstract and aggressive debate on intelligence takes place. Finally, they return to the subject:

Janice: OK now we've opened it up, now shut up and let him talk about it.

George: I have very clear reservations about the institution of marriage. I mean – I'm sorry [*laughs*].

Janice: I know, well so do I, fucking hell I've been married for nine years. I want to hear what Will's got to say about it.

George: Yes. Why are you getting married, Will?

Will: Why am I getting married, umm . . .

George: Why are you doing the legal thing, y'know involving the State and all that?

Janice: Yes that partly, yes I agree with George about all that, and I also want to know, I don't know, I want to share some of the happiness. [*Will sighs*]

George: My marriage was not the happiest point in my life.

Janice: I bet the point when you decided you were going to get married was the happy point though.

George: No.

Nicholas: There again, that's pretty hard the way you two respond. The thing is – if somebody is – It's superficial getting involved with the State, really, that's not the issue. People feel in contact and want to be together, whether they enshrine it in the form of marriage or in simply saying y'know, anointing each others genitals in champagne. I mean whatever other ritual you want, who gives a shit . . . [*Will begins . . .*]

Janice: Oh it makes a huge difference. I wouldn't still be living with Norman if we weren't married.

Nicholas: Why not?

Janice: Because it's partly that that's made everything else happen the way it has and part of the commitment is being married. [*Will tries again . . .*]

Janice: [*talking over Will and Nicholas*] I don't believe in marriage at all, no it's the way everyone has related to me as a married person.

[*After more discussion, general points, Will accusing the men of generalizing and Will being interrupted with requests to specify what he means about his prior relationship being 'everything but married':*]

> *Will:* . . . I was going to respond to what you actually said: Why does somebody decide to get married in an epoch of liberation, in which, sort of, marriage is thought to be, y'know, the moment one gets married, *one* [*sarcasm*] discovers it to be a great mistake [. . .] What you were saying is that it seems to be the dominant culture and it is something that is very strong in me and the first thing I felt, both Beverley and I felt when we decided to get married, is that we were shit scared, that's the major thing we felt, we felt we must be off our heads, we felt umm that everybody, all the people we knew well – we felt that all the people we knew would actually respond with, as it were, your type of response – you must be off your heads if you want to get married. (E3.2, G2.25–8)

The process aspect of the extract only makes sense if it is understood that there are different meanings about marriage which are held in the group and that people are positioned in relation to them. This approach is central to my use of the term discourse. To me, discourse is not just a term for whatever people happen to be saying. Rather, it requires that I specify the particular network of meanings, their heterogeneity and their effects, in this case about marriage (see Chapter 4 for a detailed example on discourses concerning sexuality). This use of the term discourse enables me to hold on to the importance of content, rather than reducing language to questions of structure and process.

Will's position in a discourse which is critical of marriage is in contradiction with the decision he has just made. Hence he (and Beverley) feared that people they knew would think they were 'off their heads'. He includes members of the group in this and, to the extent that he is correct, his difficulty in making the announcement is understandable. True George and Janice share the critique of marriage, but responses are much more varied than Will's fears anticipate. Marriage means many different things, both in the views expressed about marriage in general and more personally (for example, Nicholas saying, 'It was the only way I knew of saying, you know, that I meant what I said. You know, of putting my neck on the block'). Marriage must have meant far more to Will than the position in a discourse critical of marriage, hence the contradiction he was experiencing. In the subsequent discussion it transpires that for Will it meant a decision to have children with Beverley (also seen as an expression of intending to stay together for 15 years at least), and an expression of 'confidence in a commitment'(which was an attempt to surmount doubt). In the light of all this complexity, Will's announcement 'Beverley and I have decided to get married' is only the beginning of the story, whereas for most kinds of analysis it would be the end.

The crucial question that the extracts pose is the question of subjectivity in a theory of meaning. Will was not just at the mercy of multiple and contradictory discourses. Different positions had different effects on him which were in contradiction; for example, one position enabled him to realize his desire to have children and the other to present himself in a politically desirable and consistent light. A process analysis does have the advantage of illuminating some of these issues. But it needs to be incorporated into a theory of meaning if it is not to fall into the idealist position that I have criticized.

The example suggests how to approach the relation between discourse and meaning on the one hand and subjectivity and social relations on the other. This has a general implication for any method of analysing meaning. People's accounts are always contingent: upon available time and discourses (the regimes of truth which govern the directions in which one's thinking can go); upon the relationships within which the accounts are produced and upon the context of events recounted; upon power and the defences in operation against formulating different versions because of their self-threatening implications. The question of what subjective and intersubjective processes are involved in the production of meaning is discussed through further examples in Chapters 4 and 5. Here I should like to illustrate one particular *methodological* conclusion of a post-structuralist theory by considering the question of where one draws boundaries around the text.

Boundaries around the Text
If the theory of discourse is the idealist one that words refer unproblematically to things and sentences represent chains of logical reasoning, boundaries are not a problem. This description may seem a caricature, but take content analysis which consists of recording every instance of key words in a certain piece of text. It must be based on the assumption that words provide the essential units of meaning. Basically, structuralist and post-structuralist theories assert that meaning is based on difference – that it is achieved through relations between units of meaning or signifiers (see Chapter 4). Since those relations are never static or fixed (see below), this means that meaning is never achieved within the boundaries of a word, sentence, or even an extract. Rather it is established in an infinite network where content and context cannot be distinguished, where there is no distinction between text and the rest. The boundaries around pieces of discourse used for research purposes are based purely on pragmatic considerations.

Certainly I was aware that I brought to bear everything I knew about Will and Beverley (which was considerable) to the analysis of any single bit of text. But this raises the point that the researcher's knowledge is not exhaustive – nor, I would claim, is that of the participants themselves. A further dimension of the issue of finalizing meaning came to light when I went back to this extract 5 years later: what I know of Will and Beverley's relationship since I finished my thesis is also relevant to my understanding of the extract. Jacques Derrida has coined a concept for this aspect of meaning – 'différance' – which refers to the fact that meaning is always deferred. While structuralism grasped the capacity of meaning to extend infinitely in space (difference) at one instant, Derrida points to the extension of meaning in time.

Before I describe and illustrate this different treatment of meaning, I want to examine the methodological assumptions of feminist social psychology in the light of the points raised here.

Women's Experience and Method

In my view, the method most characteristic of feminist social psychology (and micro-sociology) is what I shall refer to as descriptive interviewing. As the interviewing method has grown in popularity (for example, the American psychologist Levinson and co-workers (1978) interviewing in the 'lifespan development' tradition), the tendency has been to present extracts which 'speak for themselves', which represent the speaker's experience. The researcher's role has been to organize this material so that it conforms to an essentially descriptive theory. The value informing the approach is typically that the researcher should not presume to question the truthfulness of the account and this position is usually coupled with the view that a person's own account is most relevant for research because it is the most meaningful to the teller. Once an account is given, it assumes the status of *the* expression of the person's experience in relation to a particular topic. What is not considered is the status of the account in relation to the infinite number of things that were not said. From my perspective, what this approach achieves is a reasonably faithful reproduction of whatever assumptions people use to interpret their own experience in the research relationship. Put another way, it reproduces (and legitimates through science) whatever discourses research participants use to position themselves at the time.

The method of descriptive interviewing represents a consistent application of the political principle that women's experience can provide a direct route to women's consciousness or identity. That principle provides the answer for feminist method: ask women directly for an account of their experience. It is also consistent with the humanistic criticism of traditional psychology that people's experience was neither sought nor valued. Again the assumption is the idealist one that the knowledge is there, based on experience, and can be represented in an account.

In this recommendation feminist research was proposing nothing new. Sue Wilkinson points out the considerable methodological similarities between feminist social psychology and ethogenics and personal construct theory. The common element is to take seriously people's accounts, rather than directly trying to measure performance or attitude. In ethogenics, this is manifest in Harré and Secord's 'open souls doctrine' and in personal construct theory in Kelly's 'first principle' (Wilkinson, 1986, p. 20). The similarity stems from the same idealist assumption, which at a deeper level is shared with orthodox psychology, that an account will produce facts whose truth-value is not problematic for the research. In other words, it is believed that an account can reflect directly that individual's experience. Some researchers are unhappy with this assumption, but the theoretical tools available to them leave them with no alternative. My starting point, in common with the post-structuralist critique of idealism, is just the opposite: people's subjectivities are produced within discourses, history and relations, and the meanings that they produce in accounts of their experience and themselves both reproduce these subjectivities and can modify them. Feminist research can, and does, help towards the emancipatory modification of these personal accounts by being sensitive to contradictions and avoidances, by exploring similarities and differences between them and by encouraging participants to go beyond abstract generalities. But to strengthen these achievements feminist method needs to go beyond a psychological theory of subjectivity and its relation to meaning to underpin its understanding of women's experience.

I know from paying close attention to myself giving accounts in a variety of different settings, that I have a stock of ready narratives to draw on which fit particular situations and which will tell me nothing new unless the person I am talking to helps me to produce something new. It can be new to me at the same time as seeming a better account of a previous experience than any previous account. I have realized that there is no context, however private and searching, which could provide the account which tells the whole truth. The number of possible accounts is infinite. In the thesis I also learned that the meanings I could generate from any given extract were theoretically limitless. The combination of this use of my own experience and the idea (from Foucault) that 'truth' is a historical product and therefore no knowledge is absolute, enabled me to begin to see participants' accounts as one production among an infinite set of possibilities.

This view shifts the theoretical goal of any analysis of discourse from one of ensuring the methodological conditions for discovery of truth to one of understanding the conditions which produce accounts and how meaning is to be produced from them. It is not that accounts are fictitious – this formulation would still be caught in the framework of belief in a truth against which fiction could be assessed. They bear some relation to events. But the relation is such a complex one that a theory of meaning incorporating personal history, culture, unconscious processes and social differences is required to make good sense of them.

Humanistic psychology and Verstehen-based sociology assume that accounts given in answer to sympathetic questioning will be an expression of the real person. Chris Weedon, in her account of feminist post-structuralism, criticizes that assumption as follows:

> The idea that it is possible to achieve self-expression of oneself as a woman, man or 'ungendered' individual in language assumes an already existing subjectivity which awaits expression. It also assumes that language is a transparent medium which expresses pre-given meaning. In radical feminism, for example, language describes the already existing natural and distorted qualities of female sexuality and of woman as mother. In this sense it is a labelling system. This perspective on language, in which it is a passive tool of communication, locates the problem of political change in the nature of the individual herself and in her struggle to find her true nature. (Weedon, 1987, pp. 82–3)

In raising these theoretical questions about the concept of women's experience, I am not suggesting that feminist methodology should not base itself in women's experience. Far from it. This book and my thesis were based on my own experience and accounts of their experience given by other women and by men. What I am arguing is that the use of the concept of women's experience as a basis for method is subject to the theoretical problems I have already discussed. It is not that there is no theory behind the concept – it is that, in the absence of an adequate understanding of subjectivity and meaning, old assumptions will govern the method. The use of an innocent-looking concept like women's experience begs all sorts of theoretical questions which have political effects. In what follows I try to show how, in contesting the objectification of research subjects, feminist theory has reinforced a different tenet of orthodox social psychological method; that the meaning of accounts is unproblematic.

Interpretation

The proposition of feminist research method, that the meaning of women's accounts is unproblematic, is partly the result of an egalitarian commitment of the researcher to the researched. It has become a point of political principle not to question women's accounts. This is the consequence of several connected developments. One is the critique of objectification which is shared by all of humanistic psychology. There is also the feminist recourse to sociological methods based on Verstehen. In common with both of the above, there is the emphasis on democracy and acting against hierarchy which are characteristic of the women's movement. The effect of this principle is that accounts must be taken to mean exactly what they say which could be dreadfully impoverishing for feminist method. It dictates that the researcher is limited to the role of setting down an organized description of what women (or whoever) say and that they cannot broach the question of what it means because it can only mean what it says and what it says reveals women for who they are. This is typical of new paradigm research which is based on humanistic premises. It can tell us a lot about women's lives, but it cannot explain women and gender. It is in danger of reproducing, rather than challenging, sexist knowledges; regimes of truth, which after all have helped to produce women's accounts of themselves and their lives. Weedon argues that consciousness-raising as a method should not be seen as a discovery of women's 'true nature', but as a way of changing our subjectivity through positioning ourselves in alternative discourses which we produce together:

> The feminist practice of consciousness-raising takes as its object women's experience of our lives. . . . [The] very process of sharing experience with other women leads to a recognition that the terms in which we understand things are not fixed. Experience is not something that language reflects. In so far as it is meaningful, experience is constituted in language. Language offers a range of ways of interpreting our lives which imply different versions of experience. . . . It is possible to transform the meaning of experience by bringing a different set of assumptions to bear on it. (Weedon, 1987, p. 85)

Participants usually strive for coherence and consistency in the narratives they produce (for research as for other purposes). This is one effect on subjectivity of the dominant Western assumption of the unitary rational subject; we attempt to construct our experience within its terms. The remainder – what is unacceptable and in contradiction – is repressed. It has effects, by being displaced through the defence mechanisms, and these effects help to reproduce the unitary rational subject. (See Chapters 4 and 5 for some detailed examples of how this works in relation to gender.) Feminist discourses have laid considerable emphasis on the contradictory character of women's experience and therefore of our identities. None the less, the principle of unitariness still underpins the vast majority of discourses, amounting to a dominant ideology which suppresses those recognitions of multiplicity and contradiction. As researchers, we are likely to go along with the dominant assumptions in the presentation of participants' accounts and this will be reinforced by our training in psychology which assumes the unitary rational subject.

Judi Marshall provides an interesting example of the problem in observing the democratic requirement to accept what her women managers said at face value. She discusses how loath she was to question the almost unanimous claim among her women manager participants, that they were not affected in their jobs by being women. In almost any social science method, if such consensus were found, it would be taken as fairly reliable fact. At first, Marshall felt obliged to believe them. However, other information in the same women's accounts appeared to contradict the claim (Marshall, 1986, p. 205). The existence of inconsistency or variability in an account is suppressed in social psychology (see Potter and Wetherell, 1987, p. 89ff.). Its recognition requires a non-unitary theory of subjectivity and its relation to meaning. In the example that Marshall discusses, her own self-understanding was implicated in how she was able to treat the women managers' claims. I discuss this in the following section.

The Researcher's Experience and the Role of Theory
Feminist researchers have rightly applied the egalitarian principle to themselves so that it is not just the experience of the women they research which requires consideration in research method, but their own experience, as women, inside and outside the research. For example, Parlee's criterion of feminist research requires that the researcher continually test her work against her own experience (1979, p. 130; quoted by Wilkinson, 1986, p. 13). Our own experience as women has been the basis of claiming a privileged position for researching women. 'Women's experience' includes us – we know about it and therefore we are better placed to understand it. Stanley and Wise (1983) make this claim explicitly when they say that only women are in possession of feminist consciousness and that only women can therefore do feminist research. But the concept of experience is too idealist to be helpful here, as is illustrated by a look at Marshall's account of her experience as researcher.

Marshall says that she was able to go with the inconsistencies in the accounts of her women managers because something in her 'experience' made her sceptical of their general claims that they were treated the same as men. What is behind this notion of her 'experience'? Initially, she implies, her response had been just the opposite – at the beginning of the research she would have been likely to go along with the women managers' claims. The forces that initially made Marshall herself resist the notion of widespread discrimination and prejudice (1986, p. 199) sound similar to those acting on the women managers. However, according to her account of her own journey into feminism, she began to recognize discrimination where before she had not seen it. Consequent changes occurred in her research so that later on, going back to the research material, she was able to recognize inconsistencies and, on the basis of those, question what might easily have been accepted as factual testimony: that these women managers did not suffer discrimination. If Marshall's 'experience' of discrimination can change into something quite opposite, the women managers' reports of their experience of discrimination must also be subject to some kind of questioning.

What Marshall's example points out is that the terms in which her women managers knew themselves (and in which she initially knew herself) were themselves a product of regimes of truth which had sexist effects – to deny the existence of discrimination. If, as social scientists, we elicit such accounts and reproduce them as fact legitimated by our 'scientific practices', we are reproducing sexist regimes of truth. In order not to do so, it is essential to ask different questions of our participants and of their accounts: for example, what forces produce the claim that they do not experience discrimination? In asking for detailed accounts of events and their responses to them, we are likely to produce information which contradicts that claim (as Marshall found in parts of her interviews).

The knowledge and experience of women researchers, as of women participants, is governed by available discourses. Marshall's experience of change was a product of the reciprocal influence of feminist discourse and other events which together shifted her resistance and facilitated her production of new knowledge. This proposition provides an important modification to Parlee's criterion of feminist research. Given the dominance of sexist regimes of truth, what ensures this consciousness? The usual answer is that women's experience of sexism does so, but women experience themselves and their relation to men through a multiplicity of discourses, many of which, as we saw in Marshall's research, do not accommodate any concept of sexism. By positioning themselves in these discourses, women can refuse to admit sexism. Consciousness is not an unmediated product of experience, because meaning intervenes, and meaning is not neutral. It has a history within power relations. When someone gives an account of her experience, some meanings are more anxiety-provoking or ego-threatening than others, and through defence mechanisms, they can be avoided. An analysis of accounts that does not acknowledge this – I am tempted to say that *avoids* it – can only reproduce knowledge that is a product of those repressions. We need to understand the ways in which the terms we use to recount our experience are not neutral, otherwise we have no sound basis on which to rest the claim that our position as women does make a difference to the research we can do. Moreover, we need this alternative theory if our own experience is to be relied upon not to be captured by orthodox knowledges which have sexist effects.

4

Making Love without Contraception: towards a Theory for Analysing Accounts

In this chapter I take two references, one verbal and one written, to making love without contraception, in order to address the difficult theoretical question of how to understand what they mean. By analysing these in detail, I try to use theory which can understand meaning and subjectivity within the same framework and provide a basis for analysing people's accounts of their experiences. One account is from a participant in my research, the other is from my own journal which I subsequently decided to use in my thesis.

In my thesis I departed from the normal procedure of separating literature review and theory building from data presentation and analysis by using two fragments early on to work through the implications of psychoanalytic and semiotic theory, and particularly of the work of Lacan. For the first time I felt I understood the utility of some of the theoretical concepts I had been struggling with by applying them to my own work. Through the use of concrete examples I could then go on to link the theory of meaning to other concepts which I had derived from my preceding critique: the notion of the non-unitary subject; of contradiction; of the relation between rational and non-rational; of discourses and how subjects are positioned in them.

When I was developing a method for interpreting texts and working out a theory of meaning and subjectivity adequate to it, I was influenced by currents of thinking which were foreign to both psychology and Anglo-American social science. These currents would now be labelled post-structuralist (see Chapter 1 for definitions, and Weedon (1987) for applications to feminism), but at the time I was drawing on what still seemed disparate trends in social theory. Post-structuralism is weak, however, on theorizing a psychological subject – a person – in relation to discourses and signification and this is where my own work concentrates.

Beverley
Beverley had recently met Will, soon after leaving a man with whom she had lived for several years. After having known each other for about a month, Beverley and Will decided, while making love one

evening, that they wanted to have a baby together and so did not use any contraception. When Beverley found she was pregnant, Will was very pleased. However, after much difficult discussion and con- fusion, Beverley decided to have an abortion. Later I asked her why, in retrospect, she had decided to make love without contraception. She said that she thought it was one in a chain of decisions which were symbols of commitment between them, in the face of worries each had about their compatibility. They had decided to live together and to get married, but neither felt dependable. Having a baby was the strongest commitment. As Will put it, it is a decision to stay together, come what may, for at least 15 years. Over a period of time I had many conversations with Beverley and Will, both of whom I knew well and whose case figures prominently in my thesis. The material I derived from taking notes is only the tip of the iceberg of my knowledge about them and their relationship.

Me

By the time that I wrote the piece in my journal which I reproduce below, I was well into my thesis, and the theoretical work I had done was informing how I made sense of my own experience, in this case a question coming up in my relationship with Jim. Jim and I had been together for over a year but did not live together. I was keen for the relationship to have a future.

> So Jim had felt reserved about us having children together, but last night I felt that had changed. I realized this at the time that I got in touch with my fantasy about making love without contraception. Jim seemed to feel we might too. We were making love and I actually felt as if it would be possible that neither of us would stop to put the cap in. That felt exciting – I think because it proved that we felt even closer – the idea of us now being sufficiently committed to each other for it to be OK to have children together. I began to recognize that we might just continue, and that it wasn't safe and started to feel worried – sufficiently worried to say so. I think the difference was because normally I can rely on Jim to take responsibility for contraception, but I sensed he was in the same space as I was. Finally it was he who said 'better put the cap in and *then* talk about it'. We did, but talking about it was different, because the question was then closed. My worry was relieved but I was also momentarily dis- appointed – not simply because, as I might have made sense of it to myself, that partly I wanted a baby (a few months ago when we thought I was pregnant it was painfully clear I didn't) but because eventually Jim did take responsibility for taking precautions (or to be accurate, I suppose we both did), and that meant maybe he wasn't so committed to our relationship after all. (E4.1, Wendy's journal, July 1980)

Signification

The central unit of meaning in these fragments is 'making love without contraception'. The question I want to explore is what this meant. At one level, it is obvious what this means; that is, what behaviour the act requires. But this is the definition of meaning I believe that psychological analysis should get away from. Psychology has behaved as if this is all there is to meaning, because it resembles fact most closely and because it coincides with psychology's premises about the unitary rational subject. I shall not try to give an exhaustive account of what this means in the two cases. To have that as my objective would be to assume that the analysis could know everything and therefore be predictive (see Chapter 2).

My intention is to illustrate the explanatory power of particular theories of meaning and how they permit links to be made between subjectivity, meaning and discourse. I start with a narrow focus, taking three specific phrases common to both accounts and then widen it, through using Lacan's conceptualization of how psychic processes are involved, and finally I consider the part played in meaning by discourse and social relations.

In the above accounts, both Beverley and I associate making love without contraception with securing commitment to the relationship (indeed, it was this similarity that first led me to its analysis). How is it possible to theorize that connection?

Rational Decision-making

It is unusual for anyone to make a connection such as making love without contraception and securing commitment to a relationship. Many would dismiss it as illogical. This position is reflected by the inability of theories of decision-making to explain it. Commonsense accounts of the issue involved in a decision whether to use contraception might be: 'Either I want a baby or I don't'; 'I can't make up my mind'; 'Parts of me want different things'. The first version denies contradictions and is based on the assumption of a unitary subject. The second similarly assumes a unitary mind, but recognizes that it is not always easy to achieve. It is based on a model of a unitary decision-maker who is dealing with external factors which are positive and negative. It assumes a rational subject by implying that once the information has been obtained and weighted, the decision will be clear.[1] The third model allows for the existence of contradictory and potentially irreconcilable parts, but these are typically divided into reasons and feelings. The implication is then that the problem is feelings and that correctness lies in a reasoned response, as in model two. A human-relations version of this last proposition would recommend expressing feelings until either they appear to form the legitimate basis for action or cease to have effects because of their de-repression.

These commonsense accounts, all associated to some extent with the dominant Western assumption of the rational unitary subject, affect Beverley's understanding of her self and her actions. For example, at the time when Beverley was still undecided about having an abortion, she said that it made her feel guilty, among other reasons, because she had 'ratted on' a conscious decision that they had made together. In that account, making love without contraception meant that she had decided that she wanted a baby and the inconsistency of deciding subsequently to have an abortion made her feel guilty. She is trying to impose unitary intentions on her actions and discount contradictory feelings.

In contrast, I did not understand my feelings through these assumptions. I had access to other discourses through which to read my responses. I was used to applying psychoanalytic concepts to interpret people's actions and by the time I wrote this, my critique of the unitary rational subject, though not consciously applied to this event, was already fairly well developed. Linked to my access to such concepts was my attempt (a joint product of human relations and psychoanalytic discourses) to get in touch with my feelings or fantasies even when these contradicted what I wanted to believe. In addition, my knowledge of how I had felt a few months previously, when I had thought I might be pregnant, helped me to be free of the 'obvious' reading of the situation which sees making love without contraception as intending to become pregnant because it scientifically entails that possibility.

Structuralist Linguistics
In order to theorize the meaning of making love without contraception in these accounts, I started off by using one of the basic tenets of structuralist linguistics which is the arbitrary nature of the sign. Structuralist linguistics is based on the rejection of a nominalist conception of language; that is, it rejects the assumption that words derive their meaning through being a direct representation of things: 'meaning is produced within language rather than reflected by language and . . . individual signs do not have intrinsic meaning but acquire meaning through the language chain and their difference within it from other signs' (Weedon, 1987, p. 23). Saussure analysed the sign in terms of its components, breaking it down into signifier and signified. For example, as in Lacan (1977, p. 151):

$$\text{SIGN} = \frac{\text{SIGNIFIER}}{\text{SIGNIFIED}} \qquad \text{e.g.} \qquad \frac{\text{TREE}}{\text{🌳}}$$

The signified here is not the object referred to, a common mistake which deprives the distinction of its analytic power by resorting to the simple duality of perceived image/object. For Saussure, the signifier is the sound or written image and the signified is the meaning.

The important point is that the separation enables the idea that the signifier is not anchored to a particular signified. Thus I have:

$$\text{SIGN} = \frac{\text{SIGNIFIER}}{\text{SIGNIFIED}} \quad \frac{\text{making love without contraception}}{\text{securing commitment to the relationship}}$$

In both Beverley's and my accounts the relationship between these two terms is established through a third term, having a baby. In both cases, the relationship between the terms is that having a baby (*h-b*) requires making love without contraception (*m-l*) but is (in part) motivated by wanting to secure commitment to the relationship (*s-c*).

The connection between *m-l* and *h-b* is one which is well-established. It is of the logical kind (assuming fertility, which we both did): if A, then B. The firmness of this connection means that meaning can easily move between the terms. I conceptualized this as an instance of metonymy, a process defined by Jakobson (1962) which refers to the movement of meaning from one signifier to another (for example, boiling the kettle). Thus (building up from the previous diagram):

$$\frac{\textit{m-l} \text{ ------------ } \textit{h-b}}{\textit{s-c}}$$

At this point I need to make a diversion into Lacan's (1977) connection between psychoanalytic theory and structuralist linguistics, because this will then enable me to address the question of how wanting to secure commitment to the relationship was expressed only indirectly through making love without contraception. In abstract terms it will insert a theory of subjectivity into the theory of meaning.

Metaphor and Metonymy, Condensation and Displacement

Lacan took Jakobson's formulation of the two basic processes of signification, metaphor and metonymy, and argued that these resembled two processes of the unconscious, condensation and displacement. Metaphor refers to the way that many meanings can be contained in one image. If instead of referring to language, we consider the ideas that are the material of the psyche, the psychoanalytic concept of condensation refers to just the same notion

– containing (condensing) many meanings in one idea or image. As Frosh (1987, p. 130) summarizes, metaphor and condensation both refer to 'the compression of multiple meanings into a single image'. This provides a dual means of conceptualizing the relationship between *m-l* and *s-c*, or the signifier and the signified. In psychoanalytic theory condensation and displacement are psychic processes (defence mechanisms) which protect the ego from uncomfortable ideas. Lacan incorporates this theory by using the idea of the signifier 'falling to the level of the signified', which in effect is synonymous with the suppression, or repression, of the signified. This accounts quite well for the status of *s-c* in the act (or fantasy) of *m-l: s-c* can remain unexpressed but it none the less signifies through *m-l*. Before raising the question of why *s-c* is suppressed – a question that takes us into the realm of discourses and power relations – I will first reintroduce the metonymic relation between *m-l* and *h-b* in order to understand how *s-c*, fallen to the level of signified, signifies through *m-l*.

Lacan sees metonymy as the same as displacement, the unconscious process whereby something of significance in an idea is detached and passed on to another image. In terms of my example, the significance of making love without contraception – securing commitment to the relationship – is displaced onto the idea of having a baby.

Lacan conceptualizes metonymy and metaphor as *axes* of language. The way I understand this usage is that it enables the focus to be on the process of connection between terms, rather than on the terms themselves. It also makes it easier to think of both axes of meaning as engaged in signification at any time. Applying this idea to build up my diagram further, *m-l* and *h-b* are connected on the metonymic axis (as I have argued above), and *s-c* signifies on the metaphoric axis, through the relation of *m-l* and *h-b* on the metonymic axis.

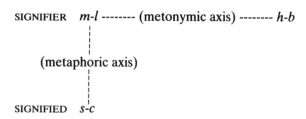

In other words, making love without contraception only means securing commitment to the relationship because it entails having a baby. When I wrote that making love without contraception 'felt exciting because it proved that we felt even closer', I was referring to meaning held on the metaphoric axis, to a partially suppressed signified (recognized through getting in touch with my feelings, rather than through a chain of logical inference) which was only possible because of the metonymic connection between making love without contraception and having a baby. Similarly, I felt disappointed, when we used contraception, because it meant that 'maybe he wasn't so committed after all'.

However, the possibility of securing commitment to the relationship does not just signify automatically through the relation of m-l to h-b. It depended on Beverley's and my understanding of the relationships we had with Will and Jim, in particular what the possibility of our getting pregnant meant for our partners. This involves looking at how meaning is established within discourses. That will also provide a way of understanding why wanting commitment to the relationship fell to the level of the signified.

Both Beverley's and my relationships were formed according to the various and contradictory prescriptions of the epoch that governed sexuality, contraception, child-bearing and monogamy. In order for my analysis of meaning to be historically located, and to cater for the uniqueness of each case, I need first to outline these various prescriptions and their relations to each other. Meaning can only be established within such a frame of reference.

This approach reflects the development of theories of meaning from structuralist premises, with their emphasis on what is static and universal, to the post-structuralist emphasis which in various ways puts history and change back into the theorization of meaning, and in so doing counters the universalizing tendencies of structuralist thought. Although Saussure made the vital move of splitting the sign into signifier and signified, he none the less maintained that meaning becomes fixed, that the signifier and signified became anchored together. The theory does not therefore account for multiplicity of meaning and changes within it. For Derrida, the critique of structuralism led to the assertion that signifiers only achieve their meaning in a specific discursive context and the fixing of meaning is achieved only temporarily as a result of this. Foucault's historical approach to discourses emphasized their multiplicity and potential contradictions at any time (for example, Foucault, 1977, 1979).

Before returning to the significance of making love without contraception, I therefore need to make another, rather long detour in order to describe discourses in relation to which Beverley and I were positioned. In my thesis I defined three discourses: the male sexual drive discourse, the have/hold discourse and the permissive discourse. These categories do not refer to actual entities. They are heuristic, that is, they are tools to help in organizing the accounts of participants and I have judged their utility and comprehensiveness accordingly. In my thesis I did not define a feminist discourse in the same way. I suppose I took it too much for granted. A feminist discourse figures in many of the accounts and it is important to give it the same status as the others. It is implicated in knowledge–power relations in the same way, although its power to define practice is limited to a small domain.

Three Discourses and their Implications

The Discourse of Male Sexual Drive
The central proposition of this discourse is that men are driven by the biological necessity to seek out (heterosexual) sex. The male sexual drive discourse has an extremely wide range of effects through the interpretation it puts on men's conduct. For example, male judges' tendency to impose lenient sentences on rapists is a result of the dominance of the male sexual drive discourse and their own identification with the position it confers on men. It is only since feminist discourse has challenged this view that sentencing is beginning – patchily – to change. (I analyse this area of effects of the discourse in relation to the trial of Peter Sutcliffe, the 'Yorkshire ripper' – Hollway (1981).)

The male sexual drive discourse relies on the more general claim that sex is natural and not mediated socially, but in practice this applies only to men's sexuality. Women's sexuality, if it is not seen as an absence in contrast to the presence of the male sexual drive, is seen as governed by the biological need to *reproduce*, rather than to have sex. A letter in *Spare Rib*, the British feminist magazine, illustrates the perseverance of the male sexual drive discourse in a man who is sympathetic to a feminist position:

> As a mature male, I am in total support of the new 'Women Against Violence Against Women' campaign with the proviso that the supporters should realise that the majority of men are decent, of reasonably high principles and respect women as equal partners in life, and only a small proportion are grossly anti-social. But, man being the animal he is, do you think that the answer to rape is well-ordered, government-run brothels to cater for the large section of single, sexually frustrated men in our society? (*Spare Rib*, 1981)

Most men's belief in the central proposition of this discourse is confirmed by their experience of their own sexuality. As Sam, one of the participants in my research said: 'I want to fuck, I *need* to fuck.

I've *always* needed and wanted . . . to fuck. From my teenage years, I've always longed after fucking.'

The Have/Hold Discourse
That sex should take place within the framework of a lasting relationship is a familiar proposition within Christian family values. Foucault contends that the 'Malthusian couple' – the heterosexual monogamous pair who had sex and stayed together in order to bring up children – was produced in discourse as an effect of the concern of governments with the analysis and control of the population. The man is head of the family and is produced as responsible for his wife and children. Since these principles are echoed in the Anglican church's marriage vows, I call this the 'have/hold' discourse.

In principle this discourse is gender-blind, and some men's sexuality is consistent with its code. However, in practice, it is applied more stringently to women (with the effect of the well-known 'double standard'). To the extent that they confer different positions for women and men, the male sexual drive discourse and the have/hold discourse are fairly complementary (as seen by their joint use in the *Spare Rib* letter). Both are longstanding and enjoy considerable hegemony. In the 1950s in Britain and other Western nations, the have/hold discourse was commonly invoked to produce the required norms of conduct in women. There was a population problem after the war and soldiers returning from the war expected their jobs back. Dr Eustace Chesser, a sexual reformer who was seen as having dangerously liberal views, argued in 1956 that 'free women' envied married women, since the sex act for women was only a prelude to satisfaction of the 'maternal instinct' and 'finding joy in family life' (quoted in Campbell, 1980). In the mid-1960s, the challenge to conventional values about sex was sufficiently strong to evoke considerable discussion. A Student Christian Movement pamphlet, for example, gave considerable thought to the position of the (Anglican) church and acknowledged: 'the teaching of the Christian church that sexual intercourse should be confined to marriage is frequently attacked as a theory and ignored in practice' (1966, p. 4).

The Permissive Discourse
By the 1960s, there was a widespread challenge in Western countries to the have/hold discourse. The cultural changes initiated by young people were broad in scope but permissive sex was identified as a central feature of what many saw as the malaise or immorality of youth. A best-seller by Vance Packard (1968) called *The Sexual Wilderness* was hailed by the British *Daily Telegraph* as being 'of capital importance for western society'. On the back cover of the Pan

edition (1968) a reviewer is quoted as summing up Packard's description of the permissive society: 'On the whole, the young of both sexes believe that they have a "right to express their sexuality in any way they choose so long as nobody is hurt".' Two features are significant in considering the relations between this and the male sexual drive discourse. First, the discourse (and this must be distinguished from its effects in practice) is gender-blind; the right to express their sexuality equally applies to the young of both sexes. It was an epoch where sex could more easily be separated from reproduction and this material change had an effect on how women were positioned in discourses concerning sexuality. That there was a change from a gender-differentiated discourse to a gender-blind discourse does not mean that women were not having pre- and extra-marital sexual relations before this epoch, neither does it mean that women were so successfully positioned by this discourse that sexual practices became gender-blind. Discourses are affected by, and have effects on, practices in a historical context. Beatrix Campbell makes the same point:

> [The permissive era] permitted sex for women too. What it did not do was defend women against the differential effects of permissiveness on men and women. . . . It was about the affirmation of young men's sexuality and promiscuity; it was indiscriminate, and their sexual object was indeterminate (so long as she was a woman). The very affirmation of sexuality was a celebration of *masculine* sexuality. (1980, pp. 1–2)

The second characteristic of the discourse is that, through it, sexuality signifies as a natural property of individuals which, because it spontaneously exists (asocially), has a right to be expressed. In this respect the permissive discourse expressed the same, biologistic assumptions as the male sexual drive discourse: whereas previously women were its objects, in the 1960s they became, in principle, equal subjects.

In the permissive discourse the sexual partner is a vehicle for sexual pleasure which is seen as intrinsic in the individual. This is similar to the male sexual drive discourse where the object is 'woman' and in contrast to the have/hold discourse where the partnership is the central principle. Reciprocity may be more evident in the permissive than in the male sexual drive discourse but it was primarily an instrumental part of improved technique. The magazine *Forum* was an influential vehicle for this discourse. Some advice from the editor in 1971 exemplifies the central assumptions behind the discourse (with the exception that, in implying that partnership is long-term, and that one goal of good technique is to avoid boredom, this quotation makes accommodations to monogamy as it features in the have/hold discourse):

> For the well-mannered lover, physical love-making has two chief aims. First you should aim to derive for yourself and your partner the greatest gratification obtainable on that occasion – in other words to take part in a reciprocal stimulation that will provide the maximum intensity of voluptuous sensations at coming off . . . Second, you should determine to acquire a skill in the technique of stimulation and a range of caresses that will allow you to change the routine of your love-making so that neither of you is ever bored when you embark on your love-making.

The biological, asocial nature of the male sexual drive discourse has been taken over, rather than challenged, by the permissive discourse: it is a logical extension of the idea that sex is purely physical, separate from social relations, unmediated by social significations. The effect of this principle is to permit the suppression of emotions concerning relationships (need, love, dependence, commitment) through their displacement on to the principle of sexual drive.

Suppressed Signification in Discourses
Beverley and I both grew up at a time when the precepts of the have/ hold discourse were being challenged, first by permissive discourse and then by feminist discourse, produced in the culture of the 1960s (specific to Western, middle-class youth) which was critical of monogamy and its surrounding institutions. Our positions within both permissive and feminist discourses recommended a rejection of marriage. (Refer back to Chapter 3 for information about Will and Beverley's decision to get married and a discussion of relevant discourses.) My own contradictory relation to this discourse was made explicit in a women's group which I tape-recorded:

> *Wendy:* Why I can't be matter-of-fact about what I want is because I've internalized – um an alternative set of values, or politics, particularly feminist politics, um, which just disagrees with that. It's not *on* to want that. It's not *on* to want to secure my future with a man even when it might change. It's not *on* to want security. It's not *on* to want to be a mother, to be into babies, to even *talk* about marriage. That's just – well it's a cop out. What would my feminist sisters say? and what my sisters say is what the feminist in me says. That's why it's so difficult because they just represent something of the contradiction inside me [*sighs*]. And that's why it feels so problematic – and why I feel so tearful. (E4.2, WG1.11)

A political position on its own, even if it is based on the recognition of its claims in one's own life, is not enough, in this account, to efface the feelings which are produced in the more traditional have/hold discourse.[2] This was a common experience in the women's movement and led to its sustained challenge to the politics associated with the old left which assumed that intellectual critique would provide sufficient grounds for personal change.

In analysing the discourses involved like this, I believe I do provide for the multiplicity and contradictions involved in meanings and desires. However, this does not in itself explain how subjectivity is involved.

Desire and the Unconscious

In Lacan's account, the metaphoric axis of signification depends on desire as the principle for the connections between signifiers and signifieds. Desire is central to his account of the infant's entry into subjectivity, which according to Lacan is simultaneous with the castration complex, the Oedipal repression of desire for the mother, the inauguration of the unconscious and the alienation of the subject with the entry into language where the child must take the position of the grammatical I, and thus enter into the symbolic realm which subsequently constructs all its relations.[3] I want to illustrate how the concept of desire can be used to understand the historical continuity of meaning through the metaphoric axis. The example is based on my relationship with Jim (though not immediately connected to the example of making love without contraception).

Desire for the Other/Mother

> I was feeling preoccupied with other things, so I suppose not paying him much attention. Jim got at me twice, about tiny things, in a way that I felt to be antagonistic. When I pointed it out we tried to do some work on it. Blank. Then he came up with the word "oranges" as if from nowhere. When he thought about it a bit he said it had something to do with his relations with women. If a woman peeled an orange for him, it showed that they cared for him. Then he said that his mother used to do it for him, even when he could do it for himself. (E4.3, Wendy's journal, May 1980)

In Lacanian terms, the signifier 'oranges', fallen to the level of the signified, is part of the metaphoric axis whose links are formed by desire. For Lacan the metaphoric axis is constituted such that its beginnings go right back through a person's history – or rather the history of their desire – entering multiple signifiers through the processes of condensation and displacement. The signifier 'oranges' connected for Jim with a suppressed signifier established early in his history through its links with desire for the unconditional love of his mother. Proof of caring in a relationship thus connected through the metaphoric axis with desire for the mother. According to Lacan, 'the desire for the Other is the desire for the mother' (Lacan, 1977, p. 286) and this is the origin of all desire.

In Lacan's usage, desire is unsatisfiable and contentless. This is the basis of its permanent ability to invade signifiers; to establish connections along the metaphoric axis, providing a continuous history of suppressed signification going back to the mother. Henriques et al. (1984, p. 217) criticized this tendency in Lacan 'to collapse into an account of a universal, albeit contradictory, subject who is not situated historically, who is tied and bound by preexisting language'. Although the Lacanian subject is fundamentally split (see Frosh, 1987, p. 132ff.), the splits bear no relation to the content of meaning nor the incompatibility between positions in different discourses. For Lacan, the *symbolic* is a monolithic system. Similarly, although Lacan recognizes that subjectivity is achieved in the context of the other, this other is also an abstract, timeless concept, not located in specific discourses and power relations. These are problems in common with all structuralist approaches. Foucault's emphasis on analysing the specificity of discourses was in response to this limitation of structuralist thought which was dominant in France.

Power, Suppression and Positions in Discourses
Discourses are always produced (reproduced or modified) specifically in relation to others. For Beverley and me the same signifier, making love without contraception, signified differently in terms of relationships with our partners, even though it was produced by the same contradictory discourses.

In Beverley's case, having a baby signified through Will's wish to have children – so much so that Beverley worried that he might only want to sustain the relationship if she too wanted a child. Deciding to make love without contraception meant, within the have/hold discourse, being the right woman for Will. This also meant that having an abortion risked losing the relationship (it meant other things too, for example, Beverley had been brought up as a Catholic). Beverley and Will both assumed that if the other wanted to have a baby, they would stay together to bring up the child and therefore the relationship would be secure. As Will often said: 'The decision to have a child is a decision to stay together come what may for 15 years.'

The 'same' relation of signifier to signified in my case actually contained a different set of implications. Its meaning has to be established in relation to Jim and the meaning which we negotiated derived from a set of discourses which we represented to each other in the relationship and which went to construct our readings of each other and of ourselves through the other. Let me specify. Earlier in our relationship, the question of having a baby had never been explicit. This was because we both presented ourselves as not wanting that kind of relationship (it was not specified, it was implicit in the particular brand of radical political discourse and lifestyle we shared). Jim was just emerging from a long monogamous relationship and presented himself as wanting the opportunity this offered to be more independent. My feminism was seen in the same light. In my journal I wrote:

> Jim perceived me as being uncomplicatedly an autonomous liberated feminist. It was painful for me to recognize the contradictions because of the guilt and it not being right-on. It nearly got me stuck in that definition. Also for the relationship it was risky (to recognize the contradiction) because that representation of myself (autonomous feminist) afforded me a lot of power. I was saying, 'I don't need men (I don't need you)'. (E4.4, Wendy's journal, Jan. 1980)

In such a situation, two people's mutual and complementary positioning in a shared discourse can seem fully to represent their identities and needs. We were both invested in maintaining those positions. Consequently, suppressed wishes, such as wanting a long-term commitment to that relationship, fell to the level of the signified.

If it was just a question of changing adherence to certain discourses in order to change one's position in them, why did I hold to a feminist discourse? There were many reasons outside my relationship with Jim, which my history had already invested with significance for my identity. I derived power through the fact that I was positioned, by both of us, in a feminist discourse. Yet faced with my position, Jim was motivated to compensate. To admit that he needed me would have been risky, not simply because our needs would then appear incompatible, but because he would have felt in an unequal position of dependence. It is in such a setting that wanting commitment to the relationship is something which signifies in suppressed ways, like making love without contraception.

Over and again in my material, I found that the positions that people took up in gender-differentiated discourses made sense in terms of their interest in gaining them enough power in relation to the other to protect their vulnerable selves (see also Hollway, 1984b). It led me to think that it was not so much desire but power which is the motor for positioning in discourses and the explanation of what is suppressed in signification (see Urwin, 1984). Certainly the relation of power and desire needs to be clarified. It's true that this kind of vulnerability is a salient feature of couple relationships because of the specific needs/desires which are bound up in them. It is also likely to be a feature of the relationships of my participants because of how I chose them and the project of challenging cultural practices, such as marriage, which contain and mask some of these anxieties. None the less, my understanding of relationships outside those between sexual partners, and outside the particular subculture of my participants, leads me to believe that the analysis has greater generality.[4] Before I turn to the theorization of anxiety and the defence mechanisms through Kleinian theory (Chapter 5), I want to give a flavour of the way that a person's history positions them in discourses and how sex can work metonymically to displace other significances in sexual relations.

Jim described his earliest memories of wanting a (sexual) relationship with a girl in the following terms:

> I remember very young – before twelve – wanting [. . .] feeling a pressure to have a girlfriend and not having a clue [. . .] I remember hanging round a local cinema thinking that might be how something happened. But it was like an abstract pressure – I just felt that I should in order to show I was growing up properly. It didn't have any connection with the rest of my life, it was just something that I felt I should – take on. (E4.5, D7.3)

This describes the effect of 'pure discourse' in the sense that an idea succeeded in affecting his actions even when there was no connection with desire or need, nor as yet with his own history. It is as if having a girlfriend still had no metaphoric links, was not connected through desire or power to other meanings. When he did get involved in the practices, it is clear that a sexual (or protosexual) relationship signified in terms of his own maturity, newly connecting up all the significance accrued during childhood of wanting to be more grown up ('be a big boy') because of the inferiorization of being younger than others.

> *Jim:* I remember, at a party – the lights went out and I found myself kissing this girl. She was rather large, rather taller than me. She was sitting on my knee, and I felt so sophisticated. I remember when I was with her another day and she said she was going to buy stockings and I felt so proud to be having a relationship with a girl who wore stockings. (E4.6, D7.3)

Having a girlfriend meant growing up and being sophisticated. It also conferred status and therefore power:

> *Jim:* At boarding school there were a lot of pressures to have a girlfriend and the more attractive – well the more rated – well yes I suppose the more attractive the girl was, the better you were for having a relationship with her. So it was just being part of a couple that mattered. (E4.7, D7.3)

As well as the tenuous and evanescent positioning as male and mature, for Jim 'Much of the relationships were actually about doing things together – having company and being able to share activities. That was good.'

The difficulty I have in using the term 'sexual relations' here is indicative of an interesting issue. So far it might seem that Jim is not talking about his adolescent sexuality, but his interests in having a girlfriend. The following passage makes the connection:

> *Jim:* I did feel the onus always to actually be pushy, to see how far it was possible to go with somebody, to see how far they were actually into me.
> *Wendy:* What did you want?
> *Jim:* Well just an obvious sign of – as a way of showing I was into them – well in a way showing I was a proper man, kind of thing. (E4.8, D7.3)

It was not a 'natural' drive that made Jim pushy, but a social one, with which Jim's developing identity as a man was bound up. He needed to prove to himself that girls were 'into him' (and that he was into them) as a way of showing that he was a 'proper man'. He did this through being (sexually) pushy because this positioned him as a proper man through the meanings given by the male sexual drive discourse. Having the simple goal of sex with a girl or woman was none the less contradictory. At the same time as wanting to get sexual to show he was a proper man, Jim was constantly held back by the fear of being rejected, 'Never making a move, let alone a pass in a relationship with a woman, unless I felt quite sure that I would actually be successful, that she would want my advances. That was very important.' Further contradictions produced his avoidance of sex in early relationships:

> *Jim:* I remember I had a very strong thing for many years that you shouldn't actually sleep with someone unless you were actually in love with them in some way. If you did it with someone you weren't in love with, it was somehow pretty horrid and pretty nasty.
> *Wendy:* To them?
> *Jim:* Well it was just, it showed you weren't – yeah, I suppose it showed the importance of sex. That it was so special that you shouldn't squander it [. . .] I never had casual sex with anyone.
> *Wendy:* Is that what you wanted, or was it a moral imperative?
> *Jim:* One reason was feeling that sex was kind of dangerous. If you had sex, it meant you were committed in some way and I didn't want that. Also that it said something – if you just had sex without a relationship, it was letting them down, 'cos you somehow thought that they'd expect a relationship and it was a pretty shitty thing to do, to have one part of it without the other. I still feel that to some extent – that somehow it was cheapening sex. It was a very prissy kind of thing, that this thing was – as I said before – so beautiful that you couldn't actually spread it around too much. (E4.9, D7.5)

Jim's account moves around between different discourses, with different positions for himself in them. Dominant is his feeling that sex should be an expression of love. Expressed by a man this is an instance of the principle of symmetrical positioning in the have/hold discourse for men and women. But the have/hold discourse does not confer symmetrical responsibility on women and men. Within its terms, commitment means taking responsibility for the woman. The signifier 'commitment' leads to Jim slipping into positioning women as the subject of the have/hold discourse, which enables him to view the woman as wanting commitment and to imply that he wanted to avoid that. His sexuality is then by default a product of the male sexual drive discourse after all – he would have wanted sex without commitment but for the fact that it would be a shitty thing to do to a *woman*. Then he returns to the previous position; sex signifies more than that to him too. He immediately derogates that position by calling it 'prissy' which, being a distinctly gendered adjective, suggests that by saying this he had put himself in the same position as a woman. To me 'prissy' also connotes taking an unreasonably high moral stance. To this extent Jim is criticizing his own feelings about sex from the position of the permissive discourse.

The meanings of sex prescribed by the male sexual drive and permissive discourses make him ambivalent about his feeling that sex was too beautiful to be casual about. In principle this is a position available to women. I have argued, however, that because gender-differentiated positions in discourses concerning sex have widespread effects, the principle does not work out in practice. The existence of gender-differentiated positions, which contribute their significance to what it means to be a man, enables him to veer away from sex signifying as too beautiful to be squandered casually. In summary, depending on which discourse Jim positions himself in, he is accorded different status – in relation to a woman and to his own masculinity. This affects the availability of different meanings in understanding his experience for the purpose of this dialogue and it is also likely to have affected his actions.

The Role of the Unconscious in Discursive Positions
The above is the discursive explanation. The following extract indicates that there is a related psychodynamic explanation, underlying his experience of sex and couple relationships, which motivates his positioning:

> *Jim:* I was frightened of strong emotions, that's basically it, 'cos I remember, again a person at school, the tremendous relief when I ended the relationship, of not actually having to be responsible for these things.

Wendy: And was it that the girl wanted to be more intimate?

Jim: Yeah. That really frightened me, 'cos I was frightened of making that kind of commitment, that kind of involvement, 'cos I thought I'd be let down, because of what happened the first time, when I was so unreserved about how I felt. I think that really affected my life incredibly, that first time when I fell in love.

Wendy: Why was having a relationship with her such a burden?

Jim: She was very strong and very emotional – that's pejorative – but I mean she had strong reactions, so that I didn't actually feel safe that I wasn't going to be knocked out, or sucked in by her. (E4.10, D7.5)

At the beginning of the extract, Jim is again taking the position of the object in the have/hold discourse, that is emphasizing the girls' needs for commitment. Then commitment slides into involvement (which in this context refers to his dependence on the woman concerned) and his account slips into his fear of being let down.[5] He felt very strong emotions the first time he fell in love unreservedly and has ever since feared the strength of his own emotions towards women he has had sexual relationships with. However, the strong emotions get projected onto the woman, so that he then fears them in her. He is frightened of hers in case they cause his defences to break down. This is an example of projection used as a defence mechanism. His own emotions, experienced as need or dependence, were defended against by projection. Jim feared strong emotions in the woman because they were the emotions that were so threatening to him that he could not acknowledge them. By projecting them onto her, he could keep them at a distance.

There is an important relation between the defence mechanism and its content. The contrast between gender-differentiated positions in the have/hold discourse and the male sexual drive discourse invite and enable Jim to position the woman, rather than himself, as the one who needs the other and wants commitment. In this area at least, gender difference in discourse parallels the effect of projection, facilitating men's suppression of their dependence on a relationship. Women may achieve such a relation in practice, but they do it without the help of a dominant discursive position. Jim was still involved in a contradiction and it was not just a result of positioning in different discourses concerning sex. The vulnerability of his identity was at stake. If he succeeded in keeping out of a relationship, he protected himself from a dependence which could be let down, but he did not get his needs met. When Jim did enter into a long-term relationship, he succeeded in doing it on power terms which tried to ensure that he would not be let down again. The experience of both Jim and Jeanette was that she was more dependent on the relationship than he. At one and the same time he retained considerable control and got his needs for acceptance and support met:

> *Wendy:* What was it that you wanted out of a stable relationship with Jeanette?
> *Jim:* Well, I think support, actually. Being able to – knowing that there was somebody who was going to be on my side [. . .] very classic. Like my parents' relationship in a way. But it was me who set the agenda. I remember – I was into classical music, so Jeanette pretended she was until she got confident enough. She was fitting in, and in a way that's what I wanted. Someone who wouldn't actually challenge me. There's a gaze of uncritical, totally accepting love that I find really attractive. I'll love forever, whatever – is a really powerful gaze. And that's a mother's gaze.
> *Wendy:* Is that how your mother relates to you?
> *Jim:* Absolutely. Whatever I do, she'll support me, she has supported me. It's quite incredible. And that makes my relationship with her very easy.
> *Wendy:* And did you get that from your father?
> *Jim:* No that was very different. Well I always felt he loved me, definitely, but he was much more – well he got annoyed with me when I didn't do it right. (E4.11, D7.6)

What is the relation between desire and power shown up by this material? Desire here is desire for the other/mother. It seems specifically about the uncritical support and acceptance which protects his potential vulnerability and quells his anxiety (for example, about not getting it right). His achievement of this is dependent on Jeanette's dependence and lack of confidence which leads her to try to be who he wants (for example, in her taste of music). Because she felt him to be stronger and she felt dependent, he could risk his own (camouflaged) dependence on her. (I spell out this argument in greater detail in Hollway, 1984a.)

Nouns like dependence imply that these qualities characterize the relationship in a static way, by implication due to personality. But in fact it was constantly reproduced between them through an unconscious dynamic process:

> *Jim:* The thing got specialized, as it were *polarized*, where *one* person does the feeling and the other person does the other parts of the relationship. And so what that means is that both sides are completely prevented from experiencing what the other person's 'job' is. Which means that you get a completely shrivelled – a completely incomplete – idea of what's going on. My relationship with Jeanette [. . .] developed in such a way that she was responsible for doing the feelings – *she* was the one that got upset, and I was the one who was *coping*, providing support, kindness, etcetera. And so what that meant was

that I didn't get to express any feelings and she didn't get to express any support. (E4.12, D6.3)

The unconscious dynamic reproduced difference. This analysis of unconscious processes which is not limited to dynamics within a person, is a crucial link between, on the one hand, gender-differentiated discourses and how they are constantly reproduced and, on the other, fundamental aspects of the psyche like anxiety or desire. The effect is of a unitary (and in Jim's case rational) subjectivity. Jim said that at the time he firmly believed that he just was not a 'feeling person'. (Whereas traditionally this would have been considered a positive characteristic, in the humanist and feminist climate of the 1970s, he felt it was negative.)

This is an example of how a signifier achieves its meaning in a discursive context, but how that meaning, when it is used by Jim to describe himself, is also a product of a specific relationship between two people whose positions are prescribed by gender-differentiated discourses, reproduced through power relations and the unconscious and motivated by desire and anxiety. There is an opposition implied between expressing feelings and giving support, which is not derived from logic. The value we are obliged to accept in order to make sense of the opposition is that people, usually women, who express feelings need support because expressing feelings is a weakness. 'Doing the feelings' is equated with 'getting upset'. Conversely, the person, usually a man, who gives support is thus obliged to position himself as someone who is strong enough not to have feelings. The logic is not contained in the opposition itself, but in the judgement attached to it, which itself is a product of patriarchal, gender-differentiated discourses. Taking up such a position recurrently in a relationship covers for his own feelings (equated with weakness, particularly in the case of a man). These meanings depend on discourses, but also they must pass through the psyche before they are reproduced. Certain meanings confer strength and thus protection, so that these will be likely to be reproduced. I explore these mechanisms in greater detail, and some more of the theory that lies behind them, in Chapter 5.

5

Relations and Subjectivity: the Case of Beverley and Will

Having developed some principles for analysis, I focus this chapter on inter-subjective relations: how discourses and meanings produce, and are reproduced by, subjectivity in the process of relations between people. The principles so far established are:

- that meaning is only achieved within the framework of discourses;
- that the multiplicity of discourses produces multiple meanings; and
- that meaning is suppressed or expressed as a consequence of its effects on the subjective experience of vulnerability and power.

Based on a single, detailed case study, in this chapter I provide a theorization of relations which provides the framework in which multiple subjectivity and difference can be understood. I draw on Melanie Klein's (1960) account of inter-psychic defences against anxiety (that is, defence mechanisms that work between people, rather than within a person).

What does having a Baby mean for Will?

Will's experience of the possibility of having a baby depends on unconscious dynamics which are primarily played out between him and Beverley, rather than intrapsychically. In the following extract he explains what effects these dynamics have on him.

Will: In a relationship for me, I mean this 'frozenness' of certain feelings is really terrible, and much more of the time than I would like, we're doing this *specialization* job. For just very split seconds, er, like on the phone – a split second in which I feel in touch with the set of feelings that I'm not normally responsible for, and that I don't particularly avow. And I don't even know I feel them. And I think, 'Shit, I actually *felt* that' and I think, I have to hold onto the *memory* of having felt it for two or three weeks. For two or three weeks I don't feel anything about it again, and I have to say, 'Well, at the moment I don't feel anything, but I *do* remember'. I mean, at one stage, Beverley said – [*sighs*] 'Well maybe we should have an abortion' and I suddenly burst into tears. Now it was very peculiar, because I – I'd actually been the person who'd been saying, 'You really should *think* about having an abortion', you know, I was giving all the excellent reasons, 'cos normally – and this might be the Catholic thing – she has always said, 'No, abortion is terrible'. Um, and for me, y'know – abortion – that's alright. It's just a matter of convenience. If she wants one. If it interferes with her studies, then we'll certainly wait two or three years. So I felt quite knowledgeable about it all and there was no problem.

Wendy: Yes, this is Will being the rational reassuring side of the relationship.

Will: Yes that's right. So it's *my job* to make her think about it. And then she actually thought about it, and she decided, maybe she would. And I burst into tears, which was completely unexpected for me. And I felt *terribly* depressed. And for that split second – it lasted about one and a half minutes for me – I knew that I actually did not want her to have an abortion. I mean, one of the things she's actually said to me is 'I don't know whether you want to have this child or not' and I've said, '*Of course* I want to have this child'.

And at one level that's certainly true. But I didn't actually feel it in the same way. And I had to hold onto that – feeling, because it went again – it went very quickly. A breakdown of that division of specialization is quite rare, and it's difficult to break out of that type of role – that division of labour. So I had to hold on to those moments of knowledge, of surprise and breakthrough. I want to *find out* what's going on, but sometimes I can't. (E5.1, G6.5)

Analysing the extract with the principles so far established, I can ask in the context of what discourses is meaning being achieved? The content of the position most accessible to Will is something like, 'I want this child, but considerations about Beverley's wider interests take priority. I don't mind about abortion and I can wait to have a child.' I shall label Will's position as coming from 'a woman's right to choose' discourse, which is a manifestation of Will's anti-sexism in the contemporary political climate. There is no single, salient, consciously affirmed discourse dictating Will's other position: 'I want a child.' His desire for a child is in contradiction with 'a woman's right to choose' in so far as Beverley is likely to decide in favour of abortion. But it is only a partial contradiction because Beverley might decide to have the baby. (I expect that if her position had been more clearly against having a baby at that time, Will's desire for a baby would have been more suppressed and he would not have been saying, 'Of course I want [this] child'.) In this example, Will's wish for a child is both articulated and suppressed: on the one hand, he can say, 'Of course I want this child'; whereas on the other, he loses touch with the feeling that he wants a baby. I see this as a common occurrence, and a phenomenon which it is important to theorize.[1]

At a rather abstract level, it can be explained in terms of the rational unitary subject prescribing norms and subjectivity. The central proposition of the discourse is that oneself should be consistent with the (internally consistent) values that one rationally upholds. Thus Will's 'I' becomes subject in a sentence such as 'I don't mind abortion' (see p. 82 for an extended discussion of this idea). It is widely acknowledged that the unitary rational subject refers particularly to men. 'Mankind' is endowed with masculine (and Western) attributes, as the noun indicates. Woman has been constructed as 'other'. This was neatly illustrated experimentally in Broverman's study which showed that the norm for normally healthy American adults closely resembled that for normally healthy American men, and contrasted with the norm for normally healthy American women (Broverman et al., 1970). In a culture whose norms, identity and conduct were not based on the premise of the unitary rational subject, it might come easily for Will to accept the contradiction between positioning himself, as a man, in the discourse of a woman's right to choose and the position of wanting a baby. But this does not explain how Will is a product of this discourse.

A psychodynamic explanation provides another part of the account: Will's anxiety is mobilized because he is not in control of the outcome. Coupled with the existence of a contradiction, this means that his desire for a child is risky. Will's unconscious defences are mobilized because of the anxiety of wanting something that he may not have and the wanting is repressed. In line with the prescription of unitary subjectivity, part of the contradiction is banished. Rationality and anxiety prescribe which part is suppressed: the part that contradicts his conscious, intentional positioning in the discourse of a woman's right to choose, which is also the wish whose outcome he does not control.

Will refers to the other domain, with which he is usually out of contact, as his 'feelings'. This is a commonplace usage derived from human relations discourse, within which 'feelings' and 'rationality' have been juxtaposed and feelings have been privileged with representing the 'real' person. I want to be careful about how I treat Will's rationalistic positions so as not to fall into the polarization of rationality and feeling or emotions. The polarization is a characteristic of Western rationalist thought and has pervaded and limited psychological theorizing. Among its many consequences, it preempts a thorough theorization of gender difference. Some parts of Will's response are outside his conscious control or intention: that is what I mean by extra-rational. As Will says (E5.2), the sort of things that Beverley says, 'which in a sense have no reason behind them . . . have a much better reason than my reason'. It was an early-established principle of Freud's work that the workings of the unconscious and mental pathology in general were not arbitrary, but based on reasons. This is why psychoanalytic theory is indispensable for dethroning rationality in the attempt to theorize subjectivity.

By looking at the production and effects of Will's rationalizing within his relationship with Beverley, I want to identify the dynamics which work between people and reproduce differences. This is an important theme in understanding the links between positions in discourse and subjectivity in a way that does not fall back into dualism. So, let me start with the evidence of how Beverley experienced him, as reported by Will. Beverley said, 'I don't know whether you want to have this child or not.' Will's response, 'Of course I want to have this child' did not convince her. Will talked in this way during the long periods when he had lost contact with what he 'actually felt', during which he relied on his memory of feeling it. I have interpreted this as repression. As a result, Beverley was not able to hear from him something that would convince her of what he 'really wanted'. What he communicated was devoid of metaphoric content.[2]

Having used the extract in order to illustrate the way a link can be made between an analysis of discourse and a psychodynamic analysis, I shall now step back from the data to explain the principles of Kleinian psychodynamic analysis.

Relational Defences against Anxiety
Three parts of Kleinian theory seemed to be helpful in understanding my research material and confirmed the analytical preferences I was already developing: the basic material for the workings of the unconscious is the capacity for projection and introjection, and thus the theory has an emphasis on relations rather than individuals; the external world is mediated through phantasy (th 'ph' spelling refers to phantasy as an unconscious process; Mitchell, 1986, p. 22), which provides an opening for a psychodynamic analysis to be linked to an understanding of meaning; the theory concentrates on processes, rather than structures, which gives it a dynamic orientation. Frosh regards it as 'a dynamic theory in the full sense of the word: one that valorizes internal forces and focuses upon the study of process. And the process which is emphasized is the intensely dialectical one of how the contradictions of the external world and the conflicts of the internal one meet, intertwine, and resolve' (1987, p. 129).

For Klein the psyche is inherently split: 'imbued with internal contradictions in its fundamental nature' (Frosh, 1987, p. 114). In contrast, mainstream object relations psychoanalysts start out by assuming a unitary subject or ego, which becomes split as a consequence of its encounters with the environment:

> In contrast to the tendency of object relations theory (to talk in terms of a return to a loss or missed state), Klein's theory focuses on the need to take

the experience of envy or destruction and make something productive out of it. [Klein] refutes a simple individualism which begins with an integrated self and then examines what the social world makes of it. (Frosh, 1987, p. 120)

However, Klein's account goes on to trace the manner in which integrity is achieved. Lately, therefore, despite the biological terminology and premises in which her theory is rooted (life and death drives and therefore the inevitability of anxiety), Kleinian theory has been taken up as having promise for a politically radical view of human nature (Frosh, 1987, p. 127ff).

For Freud, the most important defence mechanism is repression.[3] For Klein, working with very young children, the defence mechanisms of splitting, projection, introjection and projective identification are prior to this, indeed present at birth (Frosh, 1987, p. 114). The important aspect for me is that these defence mechanisms do not have as their boundary the individual psyche, but involve 'objects'. The term object in psychoanalysis does not refer to objects in the material world in the nominalist tradition that I have criticized. Initially, they are the product of the infant's phantasy world. The first object for the infant is the mother's breast which is split into the good (gratifying) object and the bad (frustrating) object. The most imporant objects are other people (or things that stand in for them) and Klein believed that these initial dynamics play a considerable part in typical adult relations (see Klein, 1960). The phantasy world is not unrelated to the real world but 'a constant and unavoidable accompaniment of real experiences, constantly interacting with them' (Segal, quoted in Frosh, 1987, p. 117). The infant's inevitable anxiety intrudes into its experience and the defence mechanisms, far from being pathological, are ego-preserving ways of coping with the threat.

Mitchell defines the relational defence mechanisms as follows:

> *Splitting* – the ego can stop the bad part of the object contaminating the good part, by dividing it, or it can split off and disown a part of itself. In fact, each kind of splitting always entails the other. In *projection* the ego fills the object with some of its own split feelings and experiences; in *introjection* it takes into itself what it perceives or experiences of the object. In [*projective identification*] the ego projects its feelings into the object which it then identifies with, becoming like the object which it has already imaginatively filled with itself. (1986, p. 20)

Splitting is defined here as a defence in its own right but, according to Klein, can also be a consequence of projection and introjection (Frosh, 1987, p. 121). I use it in the latter sense. For example, having taken up a position as a man in the discourse of 'a woman's right to choose', what was 'good' for Will was not minding and helping Beverley to do what was right for her, not imposing his own desire to have this child ('being the rational reassuring side of the relationship'). What was 'bad' was anything in contradiction to this: his desire for this child, which under the circumstances made him feel anxious and threatened his feeling of being under control. His defence against anxiety was to project his desire onto Beverley, whom he expected to want the child enough to sacrifice some of the things she was doing. This expectation was strengthened by 'the Catholic thing', the fact that Beverley had been brought up as a Catholic and, despite her feminist adherence to the discourse of 'a woman's right to choose', felt, as Will put it, that 'abortion is terrible'. For this reason she is a ready receptacle for his projections. His desire for a child, having been repressed, works through projection to seek gratification.

Will's own account in the extract of how the relationship was affecting his experience and conduct in the matter of abortion was that he was doing a 'specialization job' (later in the extract called a division of labour): that there was in him 'a set of feelings that I'm not normally responsible for' such that normally 'I don't even know I feel them'. Because Beverley is usually responsible for these, they have ceased to be part of his normal conscious experience.

Beverley interrupted the splitting by deciding that she might have an abortion and in the process she moved from being the one who minded, who thought abortion was terrible, who was worried by the whole thing. If we cease to view individuals as determining the boundaries around beliefs, positions or meanings and if we understand defence mechanisms as relational rather than intrapsychic, then it is possible to understand that multiple, potentially contradictory positions in discourses can be divided between people in a way which brings one or both of them advantages (as well as losses). Will could occupy the relatively safe, but depleted, position of not minding so long as Beverley was in charge of minding. At the first sign that she might decide to have an abortion, Will's defences were upset. Splitting is a dynamic which only becomes apparent when it is interrupted because when it is working successfully its effect is that of the unitary subject.

In this case, the split is not a simple and total one between wanting and not wanting a child: Will never entirely loses his knowledge that he wants a child. There was a more complete split occurring concerning minding and worrying on Beverley's part and not minding and reassuring on Will's. Indeed, this split between women and men came up frequently in my research material. Referring to it as projection and splitting may make it sound rather abstruse, but what

I am referring to is a common feature of relationships (I mean above and beyond the material division of labour which goes unquestioned, although the defence mechanisms would work to produce such a division). In its most obvious and practical form, if I know that my partner is 'good at' checking the oil and tyre pressures on our car, it is easy for me not to bother, to offload the responsibility (I have been on both sides of that particular dynamic). Gender obviously exacerbates this process, because men are supposed to be 'good at' cars, and women, according to the logic of difference, incapable, so that both will assume the division of labour and soon it will be the case, unless a different discourse intervenes to interrupt them. The difference about the dynamics I am talking about here is that they are not within conscious control: it is not corrected by saying, 'I'll check the car from now on' (if that works – forgetting can be a powerful device of the unconscious). Will was not able to remake contact with his sure knowledge that he wanted a child until Beverley changed her position, thereby interrupting his position, which was dependent on it.

The following extract specifically relates to Will's rationalistic mode of communication. I have interpreted this as part of a defence, using evidence of what happens when Beverley interrupts it. Through it I look at the effects it has, namely to produce Will to himself as strong by projecting his weakness:

Will: We were having a conversation about something or other which at the moment I've repressed. But – um – oh yes, it was about the small matter of pregnancy and having a child. I can't imagine how I forgot that [*laughs*]. And I was in a sort of reassuring mode [*George:* Right] and what she said was she was very worried about it, and I said, 'well' – it was at the end of quite a long conversation and she'd been saying how she felt and I'd been doing, I'd been doing my reassuring bit [*laughs*]. It sounds so ludicrous but it wasn't at all. Umm: 'In my mind, I'm prepared for every eventuality', right. And this was some way of saying 'If you want an abortion, we'll have an abortion, and if you don't want an abortion, we *won't* have an abortion. Y'know I'm prepared for every eventuality.' And she said quite sharply and nastily, 'You mean we could have the child and then strangle it immediately afterwards'. And um [*laughs*] I burst into tears, um, because, and it was very strange because what her saying that meant was 'You've been talking in a completely abstract way, as it were without any sensations whatsoever'. And actually that got me out of my reassuring algebraic thing – like 'We are prepared for every eventuality'. And I'd actually felt all that and I'd also felt quite distant. I felt I was the reassuring one, y'know, I was feeling anxious for myself, yes, but she was much more anxious and therefore I had to say we were prepared bla bla. And that sharp remark – and she didn't know why it was – it just tore away that um that sheath over my emotions. That sheath of being in charge of patriarchal reassurance.

Sarah: Why are *you* in charge of it?

Will: 'Cos I'm in charge of the universe and I have to look after her! [*Janice laughs*] It was very *strange* 'cos, like it felt like a tearing away of something that I hadn't realized was there. I just burst into tears, and that's – actually usually . . . That's one of the very important reasons why I value my relationship with Beverley because she will say things like that which in a sense have no reason behind them. Y'know – they obviously have a much better reason than my reason – and tear that away. Er – and I don't even notice I'm in it.

George: You mean you're intellectualizing.

Wendy: But that, that's a power trip. I mean I really empathize with that, because the thing about 'don't worry – I'm not feeling these anxieties for myself. You're feeling the anxieties. And I'm telling you that – I'll look after you.' [*Will:* It'll be alright] I mean I'd just hate it, I mean I'm not reacting to you, y'know, but just the way it goes on so often [. . .]

Will: But the point is that my deflection is that if anything makes me feel that somebody else – and it's incredibly easy for me to feel that somebody else's needs or fears or anxieties are greater than mine – I immediately shift into this caring thing.

Sarah: Yeah but, can you stop there a minute? Because do you *really* feel that theirs is greater than yours?

Will: I don't know. But certainly – that's, I don't know whether it's *true*, I always tend to think that other people's needs to talk or needs to work things out are greater than my own. Because in a sense I have this fantasy of myself as quite strong. (E5.2, G4.8–9)

Before going on to emphasize the unconscious dynamics involved – which is the main theme of my argument at this point – let me put Will's statement, 'I'm in charge of the universe and I have to look after her' in its discursive context. The statement may be a joke about his omnipotent/patriarchal tendencies, but it is also the position that the have/hold discourse, and its many cultural parallels, prescribes for men. As head of the family, they are responsible for the 'universe' of their women and children. These historical forces are at work in Will, explaining the unilateral position of reassurance. It is important to bear in mind this discursive force in the psychodynamic processes which I emphasize in what follows.

Will's articulation of his position has been depleted of the signification contained in the metaphoric axis to such an extent that he is left with an abstract, algebraic sentence: 'In my mind I'm prepared for every eventuality.' The effect of saying this is to communicate 'without any sensations whatsoever'. It is also to leave him feeling 'quite distant'. His communications left Beverley not knowing whether he really wanted the child (interposing here were probably her own doubts and projections onto Will). As Mandy wrote in her journal, faced with a similar position in the man she was having a relationship with: 'If he's saying he has no expectations, no needs, then I can't let him down. If I can't let him down, he has more power: he has the power to hurt me, but I don't have the power to hurt him.' In a note Beverley wrote later in response to reading a draft of some of the thesis material, she wrote that she wanted him to be 'completely unambivalent' about wanting the child. She got this information when he burst into tears ('For that split second, I knew that I actually did not want her to have an abortion') and it changed the power between them to a position where they both knew that Will needed something from Beverley. I have already argued in Chapter 4 that suppressed in the act of making love without contraception (an act for which they were both responsible) was her desire for proof of Will's commitment to the relationship. Now that she is pregnant, this suppressed signifier has moved to another location (Lacan referred to this as 'the homelessness of desire').

In order to know, she needed his uncontrolled, undefended response. In the first extract, she achieved this by taking up the opposite position from the one that Will expected and from the one that secured his not minding. In the second extract she says something which cuts through his abstraction; which showed it up as meaningless. The idea of strangling their baby at birth transforms an abstract pregnancy into a living baby, his child, and he bursts into tears. For a moment the problem assumes its full significance.

My analysis of the first extract makes the link between positions in discourses, contradiction and repression of the unacceptable or bad and the relational defence mechanisms and anxiety. But it did not address the issue of subjectivity. By the end of the last extract, Will seemed to arrive at a fundamental issue for his subjectivity; the net effect of these dynamics, despite what he dislikes, is that he ends up feeling 'quite strong'. True, he implies that this is the cause of his urge to 'shift into this caring thing'. In any discourse analysis which takes account of unconscious dynamics, this cannot be simply accepted. Rather than look at strength as a characteristic which Will has, I look at it in terms of an effect he achieves through relational dynamics, backed up by pre-established meanings and positions available in discourses. In this case Will's 'caring' positions the other person as having greater needs than himself, which for him is equivalent to being strong in comparison to the other.

Supposing that he *does* have needs (supposing that everybody does), how does he feel about them? He implies that having needs signifies weakness. That he is uncomfortable about acknowledging his own needs is supported by something Will says during the weekend when he is talking to David, the only man there who is his age or older:

> *Will:* Yeah, you feel that. Now you see, I feel that in spades. If I fight, I fight from the wrong side. So I am constantly feeling – I mean this is exaggerated but – like an elephant walking around with lots of eggshells, and I hate people for being eggshells. And I hate myself for being an elephant. Like, I could hit very hard at you [*to David*] because you're a man. And also because you're my age or older. And I feel you can *take* that. I've not in any way tried to be kind to you. My thinking about kindness is that I really *distrust* – I really fight feeling very kind to lots of people, because I feel it puts them in an inferior position by not telling them what I think, by being diplomatic, and all the rest of it. When people were kind to me in that way, I used to lap it up, and hate me for needing it . . . and them. (E5.3, W9.5)

Before, Will acknowledged that he positioned people as inferior, but now he says he hates people for being so positioned, for being eggshells that the elephant inexorably tramples. The dynamic is not simply a response to how people act towards him, but one already indicated by some of the dimensions of social (and power) difference – sex and age. But there is no simple determination of their relative positions as a result of these dimensions; Will reproduces his positioning as an older man (despite hating himself for it) because of his own fear of being rendered inferior by kindness. For him there is no exercise of kindness independent of a power relation: either you care for somebody else, retaining your strength, power and control by not needing care, or you are made inferior by having needs. A further extract, where Beverley is also in the group, illustrates the cost of Will's need to position himself as caring and supporting:

> *Will:* There is a sense in which I feel – and this comes back to teaching, and it goes back a hell of a long way, to a sort of elder brother reassurance – comforting – this sort of thing. And um, like I feel, and I *do* feel that it is a strain, um, both a strain – no I do feel it as a strain. But in a sense, when you [*to Beverley*] say things like, 'Well I just can't afford to mother you . . . at the moment', somehow that's a very powerful instruction – you may not mean it as a powerful instruction, but it triggers off a whole set of – um – like primary programme in me, which I feel that in general I'm trying to overcome, and that reminds me of what my proper role is. And my proper role is not to need comforting. [. . .] You once said that you like it – when I got confused or uncertain, and stopped as it were being sort of this unilateral comforter and reassurer. And the other thing you did say was – and not on the same evening – that this moment in your life, etcetera.
> *Beverley:* Well I wouldn't equate the two things somehow, but when you *are* confused, it doesn't seem to me that you need mothering. They're just two very different things. And the similarity is in the sort of masculine image of actually *knowing* where you're at, so well. Y'know, and not having any confusion – any cracks at all. And er not actually needing support. (E5.4, G5.8–9)

It is a strain (or something worse that he holds back from saying) for Will to be unilateral comforter and reassurer because, as the adjective indicates, it excludes him from getting caring back: receiving caring ('mothering') from Beverley is proscribed.

Will connects feeling confused with the issue of getting his needs met, although there is no obvious connection. According to Beverley it is because both states (confusion and neediness) undermine his need to have 'no cracks at all'. Her interpretation is supported by my argument that, for Will and others, strength entails repressing needs entirely. But to say that they are repressed, rather than non-existent, is to say that they have effects. There seem to be two related sets of effects, both of which involve Beverley. The first is that Beverley is (partly) produced as helpless and weak. The second is that Beverley protects Will from his own vulnerability.

The effect of Will's support and caring (which included total financial support as well as a great deal of domestic work) was to produce in Beverley the experience of helplessness:

> *Beverley:* I really feel like my life's being made too easy for me, and I've turned into a kind of – I've turned incredibly lazy because of it. No really, yes, and that's one of the reasons – I feel completely weak and helpless. I feel like when I'm around you, I lose all resolve. I do. (*Will:* Yep] But I mean, I don't know why it happens, why I let it happen. (E5.5, G5.5)

Will's power to succeed in the projection is dependent on some part of Beverley – the dynamic is one in which Beverley participates. This produces a circular effect between two people which makes the reproduction of a dynamic all the more difficult to change. The projection dovetailed with parts of Beverley which meant that she positioned herself in a complementary way. This is not to say that it was a part of Beverley's 'character', indeed she felt extremely contradictory about what she began to experience as her helplessness. In her previous relationship:

> *Beverley:* I just lived eight years with a man that I fucking mothered the life out of, y'know, [*Will:* Mm] y'know, paid his rent, fed him, and – I mean – that's not what you want, but like, it just makes me *scream*, the thought of it, like if any of us is going to be like that – that bloody helpless, dependent, grown human being. (E5.6, G5.5)

This is one reason why 'mothering' signifies in such negative ways for Beverley (another is the hurt that she experienced receiving at the hands of her own mother).

Will was first attracted to Beverley, and she to him, when she was in a 'problem situation', which meant that she was grateful for his caring and support. But now the dynamic is something in which they both collaborate:

> *Will:* I don't think I'm inventing a complication that isn't there.
> *Beverley:* In that sense you *are* though. What I said three months back – that came out of such a – a sort of problem situation, that I'd just like to ignore it. But you're still mostly *using* that as your way of looking at me, aren't you? I mean, I mean, I was like a baby then, wasn't I?
> *Will:* Well I don't know. One of the problems we've said – is that I don't know, I haven't known you much, and we've got to know each other properly within the period where you were like most helpless. But in a way I need – I suppose what *is* true is that I need quite clear counter-statements before I know that you are *different.* [*Beverley:* But . . .] No, but take, for example, sleeping on your own – sleeping at nights.
> *Beverley:* But it's funny because – it was really nice having two nights on my own.
> *Will:* But you didn't say that.
> *Beverley:* No you said to me, 'How did you sleep?'
> *Will:* [*talking over*] What you said to me was you couldn't sleep.
> *Beverley:* Yes but that's not what I *meant.*
> *Will:* Yes but what I heard was, as it were, 'I didn't sleep very well' and I therefore felt . . .
> *Wendy:* Why didn't you tell Will that you actually enjoyed two nights on your own?
> *Beverley:* Cos I didn't want to hurt him. [*All three laugh.*]
> *Wendy:* There you are you see. You both end up doing something that won't suit either of you, for the sake of some notion about what you should do for *love.*
> *Beverley:* Well because I've felt so uncaring lately, and hard-hearted and things, I thought I can't . . . put that on top of it all . . .
> *Will:* Can't tell the truth. (E5.7, G5.8)

Beverley colluded in being treated as needing Will to be there for her. She implies that he would be hurt if she behaved as if she did not need him. The effect was to continue being positioned as helpless, which had all sorts of advantages of care and protection which Beverley did not want to lose. On the other hand, being in need of help signified for Will as her being weak and he hated people being weak.[4]

Signification of the Repressed
The splitting of strength and weakness was not entirely successful. If it had been, Beverley would not have been reluctant to hurt Will. It was as if she knew that Will's feeling of strength depended on being needed. In the following extract, the relation between Will's vulnerability and his position is indicated. Will has just said that Beverley is not physically expressive to him and he reads this as an example of her not caring for him.

Sarah: Well you're not being very honest, Beverley. You're going to have to tell him to piss off. I mean, you can *say* that – that you don't like being cuddled. I mean – he'll stand it. He's not going to crumble, are you?

Will: I don't think so. It'll probably be very good for me.

Beverley: No that's right. That's what I'm very *frightened* about – your vulnerability.

Will: I'm just frightened by your dishonesty [*laughs*] – that's what frightens me.

Beverley: Well it's because it's part of this thing about mothering – when you say that you're a bit confused, and that means mothering. It seems to me like you're saying, if you admit anything that's a contradiction, that you'll completely fall apart.

Will: I have difficulties in being vulnerable – anyway. And that's because you've said, that you haven't got much energy at the moment for doing things for other people – um, and you're frightened of my vulnerability, because you're afraid I'll fall apart.

Beverley: 'Cos *confusion* is a *state of being* for me. I'm afraid that you don't know yourself. Like that thing about biting. You don't dare bite, or something like that, because you feel you'll go berserk. So I suppose in a way I've felt that you think lurking beneath you is this *thing* – who knows what it is, sort of thing. And if you're frightened of it, then I'm even more frightened.

Will: And if you're more frightened, then I have to restrain it.

Sarah: Oh come on, restraining it is part of who you are anyway. (E5.8, G5.11–12)

The suppressed signification in Will's relation to asking for support or being confused is picked up by Beverley; that is she reads what he says with due recognition of the metaphoric axis, even though he maintains, 'I don't think I'll fall apart'. She recognizes this through its difference from her own relation to confusion. For her it is a 'state of being', whereas the suppressed signification in Will's position, as Beverley reads it, is that if he admits anything contradictory, he'll fall apart because it's too threatening.

There is a principle in psychoanalysis that the energy with which a defence is maintained is equivalent to the energy of the original repressed desire: it's a version of 'Methinks the lady doth protest too much'. People's vulnerabilities often signify through the energy with which they are protected, and the positions people try to occupy can indicate the opposite. Beverley reads the extent of Will's vulnerability through his heavy suppression of it and it therefore appears as particularly threatening. So Beverley colludes in Will's positioning himself as the giver of support because that way they are both spared his vulnerability. Her unspoken fear is that if she does not, he would become dependent (possibly his fear is that then she would reject him).

In Charlotte and George's case (Hollway, 1982, pp. 411–21) a similar dynamic was in operation. Charlotte was attracted to George as an older man who could support her. She gradually read the same signs as Beverley is referring to and, not for the first time, her attraction dissolved as she began to feel that he was 'a potential needer', rather than someone on whom she could depend. The effect was circular because George felt even more obliged not to express his vulnerability, which she then picked up through its suppression in signification. All this took place without these feelings being expressed between them. If this is common (and I believe it is), referring back to the triangular relationship of father–mother–child which is fundamental for both Freud and Lacan, men's reluctance to show vulnerability is grounded in the relational dynamic, rather than being the simple product of an intra-psychic defence against anxiety.

Beverley feels she can handle confusion, strong feelings and being positioned as weak. Because she knows confusion (it is 'a state of being'), she is not so afraid of it – the known is never so frightening as the unfamiliar, especially when one's fears are displaced onto the unfamiliar. A further reason is that women are more readily positioned in this way in heterosexual relations, because of the gender-differentiation in discourses. This may contribute to the dynamic in Will and Beverley's case, but it could not provide an account on its own. In Chapter 4, when I was commenting on my own experience, I reported the opposite; that is, I needed to avoid showing my feelings, crying, etc., *because* it would position me in a way which was evaluated negatively. One of the reasons I have spent so much time on Will's case, and why I have been able to derive so much from it (apart from the fact that his account was rich in potential for my interpretation), is that I recognize my own style of defence in Will's case. That is worth recording here in case the implications for gender difference are drawn too hastily at this point. None the less, what is different for Will and me is the availability of positions in gender-differentiated discourses such as men's responsibility in the traditional have/hold discourse.

Method

In a sense, the whole book up to this point provides an illustration of what the alternative theory requires of discourse analysis. The first extract in this chapter serves to illustrate some basic principles.

It is not a typical account of a difficult decision in somebody's life. (In Chapter 4, I summarized the typical lines which accounts of decision-making follow.) It is not just that statistically based psychological methods could not produce such an account – that much is obvious. Even in an in-depth interviewing situation, it is quite difficult to produce an account which acknowledges contradictions, describes the detail and diversity of events and analyses experience in terms which go beyond the unitary, rational subject. It is evident from what Will says that the account most accessible to him would normally have been the one which he sums up as 'I felt quite knowledgeable about it all and there was no problem'. He would not have been engaged in 'faking', as social psychology would have it; rather, the account would have reflected the limits imposed by his own defences, which most of the time he could not break through ('I want to find out, but sometimes I can't').

These affect not only what he can say, but what he knows himself about what he wants. They exist not within him as an individual, but between him and Beverley and within the research group. Therefore, the framework of analysis must embrace intersubjective relations.

Will was able to go beyond the comfortable, obvious account because of various influences, some outside and some within the research. First, for some time Will has moved in networks where it is taken for granted that he will speak and act within the meanings produced by feminist discourse. Second, and in consequence, his relationship with Beverley kept him in touch with his contradictions and also gave him some new concepts through which to understand it. (For example, Beverley pointed out that it was she who first used the metaphor 'sheath over his emotions' about Will's position (E5.2). This indicates how some of the consciousness-raising work that was done within couples affects their accounts in the research. It was most common for men to learn this from women, and it was a part of the effects of feminist practice at the time.) Third, Will had been quite active in humanistic groups whose general aim was self-knowledge (this is one reason why the term 'feelings' figures so large in his account). Finally, my approach was based on exploring contradictions and keeping the focus on relations, rather than individuals. I reflected that in how I talked about my own issues and the comments I made about what others were saying (for example, 'Yes, this is Will being the rational, reassuring side of the relationship'). To do this I was already making use of the concepts I had developed; in this case, the idea of splitting informed what I said, although I did not use the term. Since I knew Will well, my approach already informed his understanding of the issues, outside the research. I was not the only one making these kinds of interventions (for example, Sarah in this chapter) – they were part of the assumptions common to most of the participants, many of which could be said to emanate from a feminist discourse which was dominant in that network. These are some of the most obvious conditions for the production of research material in Will's case. In other conditions, the accounts resulting from research interviews will differ. For example, decision-makers in organizations are likely to understand the interview to be in the context of their jobs and will reflect individualist assumptions by talking about themselves, their ideas and actions. As Evelyn Fox Keller (1985, p. 9) puts it: 'Men's lives are apersonal *because* and to the extent that women's lives are personal'.

The Human Subject, Subject Effect and Subjectivity

In this final section I want to review the implications of the interpretative analysis in this chapter for a theory of subjectivity. In Will's rationalizing mode we saw the effect of his taking up a position in language/discourse (I use both terms here because as I shall show, they lead to different emphases in the analysis). The effect was to place Will as the subject of a claim 'I don't mind (if Beverley has an abortion)'. A Lacanian analysis fits this material well:

> For Lacan, the human subject is constructed in and through language. This does not imply that there is any particular pre-existent subjectivity which learns to express itself in the words made available to it by language, but rather that the initially 'absent' subject becomes concrete through its positioning in a meaning-system which is ontologically prior to it and more extensive than it. The subject, the pronominal 'I', is created through an order that originates outside it, in the flux of inter-subjective relationships that surround it and elect it to a place in their midst. Because of this, we are possessed and 'spoken' by language we do not own ourselves, but are constructed according to the possibilities offered us by words. (Frosh, 1987, p. 130)

For Lacan the subject is formed through the process of two developmental splits, both of which are based on an illusion of integrity. Lacan, therefore, refers to a 'subject effect' as a way of denying the integrated subject which is the basis of humanistic discourse.

The first split comes with the infant's perception of unity through the way that s/he is related to as integrated. Lacan calls this the 'Mirror phase'[5] in which:

> The child's perception of her/himself in the mirror (that is the gaze or responses of the other with whom the child interacts) leads to a joyful but mistaken perception of bodily unity as the site of a unified self, a parody of all essentialist theories of psychology. (Frosh, 1987, pp. 132–3)

The perception is a fiction which produces the effect of subjectivity through the child 'identifying with a vision that comes from elsewhere' (1987, p. 133). The second developmental split occurs when the child enters language, taking up the position of the pronominal 'I': 'I identify myself in language, but only by losing myself in it like an object' (Lacan, quoted in Frosh, 1987, p. 134). These splittings produce the human subject, which for Lacan is no more than the 'subject effect'. While this is an important and necessary alternative to the subject of humanism, and rightly emphasizes the production of the subject in language, it cannot account for the fact of change. Frosh concludes:

> Many have criticized Lacan for the totalitarian implications of his work: if humanism is a fraud and there is no fundamental human entity that is to be valued in each person, one is left with no way of defending the 'basic rights' of the individual, for the individual is apparently nothing more than her/his construction. (1987, p. 137)

The reason for Lacan's conclusion is his abstract view of language or 'the Symbolic', which derives from his 'relentless structuralism' (Frosh, 1987, p. 137). The specific and multiple content of language disappears to be replaced by universal claims about 'the Law of the Father' which covers the whole realm of the symbolic with its signification. In *Changing the Subject*, Cathy Urwin's summary proposed that:

> Instead of prioritizing the symbolic order with its universalist and timeless implications, we might prioritize instead the discursive order of particular discourses, viewed in their historical specificity. Following the post-structuralist emphasis on the production of modern subject forms through social apparatuses, here we are focusing on the ways in which language is implicated in the production of particular regimes of truth, associated with the regulation of specific social practices. (1984, pp. 279–80)

By using the Foucauldian notion of discourse, as I showed in Chapter 4, an analysis can deal in detail with the multiple content of language, the effects of taking up different positions in discourses, the meanings that they confer, and the differential values these entail for different categories of people. This enables me to incorporate, as does Foucault, the continuous and mutual relation between knowledge (discourses) and power. In the example of Will's position 'I don't mind (if Beverley has an abortion)', a Lacanian analysis would emphasize the 'I' in language in general. In contrast, the specification of the discourse of 'a woman's right to choose' in the context of other contradictory discourses (for example, what Will refers to as 'the Catholic thing') enabled me to detail the effects on each other through the power of their positions in discourses.

However, having moved back into a Foucauldian discourse analysis, what gets lost is a psychodynamic account of the subject. In Foucault, the subject is a product of discourses. This is an improvement on the notion of the individual as a set of roles, because multiplicity, contradiction, change and power are at the heart of a Foucauldian analysis. But it does not account for what we experience as individuality: the fact of each person's uniqueness in relation to language/discourse.

Once the content is put back into language, Lacan's account, which places desire at the centre of signification as I illustrated in Chapter 4, can be used to make the links between discourse and subjectivity. On the metonymic axis, signification may reproduce language or discourse which is normal for the (sub)culture, for example, Will's position of not minding about abortion. But on the metaphoric axis, signification is unique to each person, because at every point in their history, meanings have been invested by desire (for example, how 'oranges' signified to Jim in a particular context – Chapter 4). Desire does not follow generalizable routes, and its logic is not that of the rational subject, because unconscious processes work through displacement and condensation.

These concepts contributed to my understanding of Will's rationalizing mode. In my thesis I took it further and argued that subjectivity can be theorized as a special case of signification – self-signification so to speak – whereby the metonymic axis encapsulates the normative products of discourse/language and the metaphoric axis encapsulates the specific history of desire as it successively invades significations and invests them with the interests of the ego.

What I did not succeed in doing was to integrate my use of Kleinian analysis properly into this. The 'other' is a feature of Lacan's explanation, but it seems often to refer to everything that is not the subject. It is true that intersubjective relations feature centrally in Lacan's theory: the Oedipal situation involves recognizing the importance of the triangular dynamic between father, mother and child. But because this is treated as a moment in childhood, the effect of a universal structure, the theory becomes static. (Another effect is that gender difference is theorized as a product of Oedipus and the castration complex, without taking the tortuous, but in my view necessary, route through the continuous, everyday, defensive negotiation of intersubjective relationships within the field of effects of power/knowledge relations.)

This is where Klein comes in. Because she privileges the defence mechanisms which work between people rather than within a person, intersubjective relations become the location for the negotiation of meaning and its effects, through power, on subjectivity. These relationships are always the product of two or more people's unique histories, the contradictions between meanings (suppressed and expressed), differentiated positions in available discourses, the flux of their continuously renegotiated power relations and the effect of their defence mechanisms. Thus they are never simply determined, either by the intentions of those involved, or by language/discourse.

Nor, however, are the relationships and their effects on subjectivity arbitrary. In the analysis of Will's case, as of those in Chapter 5, the principle motivating the taking-up of positions and the mobilizing of defences, was the vulnerability of what psychoanalysis calls the ego. According to Klein, this vulnerability is an unavoidable effect of human nature; anxiety is the original state of human nature. I think there is probably a way of giving anxiety a suitably central role in a theory of subjectivity without Klein's resort to human nature. The way that the infant is positioned by adults, as a result of their anxieties, defence mechanisms and power relations, as well as their access to differentiated positions in discourses, means that anxiety for human infants can be culturally inevitable, rather than naturally so. The continuous attempt to manage anxiety, to protect oneself, is never finally accomplished (though mature adulthood can achieve relative stability and a state of apparent peace with anxiety). Anxiety thus provides a continuous, more or less driven, motive for the negotiation of power in relations. This seems to me a more likely version of what is unsatisfiable and pervades signification and action than Lacan's desire with its resort to a Freudian notion of sexuality.[6] Urwin took empirical child-observation material as the basis for her re-analysis of the 'Mirror' phase. She concludes: 'taken together, these examples imply that power relations interpenetrate the production and reproduction of subjectivity throughout children's development' (1984, p. 285).

Frosh concludes his discussion of the implications of Lacan for feminist theory by arguing that Lacanian theory needs to take into account those power relations which construct the system itself. My analysis has taken only those aspects of power relations which are produced and reproduced in discourse, but of course these are related to material structures and practices. In the thesis I discussed their links to the power relations produced by material inequalities between men and women. Socialist feminism has always strongly emphasized the importance of not reducing power relations to psychology. However, the issue concerning power in heterosexual relations for some (salary-earning) feminists, myself among them, had returned to how subjectivity was not a direct or immediate effect of material power relations. I was interested in how, despite my financial independence, my ownership of a flat and a car, my greater age, occupational status and earning capacity (and despite the effect that this certainly had on the man with whom I was having a relationship), power was more than these things: it was always dynamic and two-way and tied to the extra-rational forces which here I conceptualize through the notion of anxiety and the intersubjective defence mechanisms.

The effect of all this for a theory of subjectivity can best be exemplified by returning to Will's case. Taking up the pronominal 'I' in 'I don't mind (if Beverley has an abortion)' was only the first level of analysis. It did effect an alienation ('I felt quite distant') but that was not an inevitable and static state of affairs. It was only one part of a contradiction, the outlines of which were provided by discourses and the positions available through them. It was also the effect of a process which, while not in Will's conscious control, was a continuing achievement of his defence mechanisms. These were motivated by Will's vulnerability, his need to reproduce the effect of appearing to himself as stronger than other people. Since the major defence mechanism in operation was projection, Will's achievement was always dependent on someone else – a state of affairs which came to light when Beverley interrupted it. It was in this sense unstable. It was also unstable in the sense that his achievement of appearing to himself relatively strong was at the cost of another quite insistent need – to be cared for, or 'mothered'.

Just as the metonymic axis is not all there is to signification, though it can be all that is apparent, so the subject effect is not the whole story of subjectivity. What is left out of the subject effect is what is suppressed; what – to follow the parallel – has fallen to the level of the signified. This would mean that it still has effects. For example, though Will suppresses his desire for a child, in order for his position within the discourse of a woman's right to choose to be paramount, the effects are still felt of the splitting and of his unconscious projection of the suppressed into Beverley – as long as this dynamic works to hold Beverley in position, Will can get his desires fulfilled.

By subjectivity, I want to include the multiple and contradictory forces which affect practice, even when these are not available to a person's experience at any given moment (or in principle, ever). These other forces will still have their effects: on power relations, on subjectivities, on positions in discourses and practices and thus on the reproduction of certain knowledges and not others. All of this means that my concept of subjectivity is not only dynamic, non-unitary and embraces the extra-rational, but it is *discoverable only within inter-subjective relations*. In the final chapters of the book, I show how this analysis can be applied to the particular case of the production of psychological knowledge, revealing the part played by gender difference.

6

How did Psychology come to be what it is?

In the preceding two chapters – the ones that actually do the new theoretical work towards a theory of subjectivity and a method adequate to it – I have departed radically from the principles of psychology, both in respect of theory and method. Much of my earlier discussion indicated why I came to believe that this was necessary. But why has psychology gone in the direction it has? What forces have shaped it in such a way that it could not offer any plausible basis for answering the questions I was trying to ask? If we are to develop alternatives of the kind I am suggesting, it is necessary to ask why and how psychology came to be what it is, because unless these forces are understood, we cannot appreciate how they shape the alternatives too. Since my concern is primarily the alternative psychology of gender, I return to the question of how these historical forces are limiting feminist social psychology. In Chapter 3 I discussed its method, whereas in this chapter I shall discuss its theoretical base.

Speaking of psychology in the singular can be justified by reference to some of its most dominant principles, particularly its status as a science and its assumptions about the nature of the individual. However, it is also very disparate. I discuss four rather different psychologies: behaviourism, psychometrics, human relations (or humanistic) and social psychology, which I believe have had the most important effects on psychological practice. It is not my intention to give a detailed history, but rather to illustrate the theme of power/ knowledge relations in psychology.

The orthodox answer to the question 'How did psychology come to be what it is?' is that psychology is a science and, as such, is guaranteed through its methods progress towards knowledge of that part of nature that it takes for its object. This begs a supplementary question, however, a question on the terrain of philosophy of science that would probably not be thought to be at issue in orthodox psychology: what is the character of that knowledge and how can we know that science guarantees its truthfulness?

Psychology as a discipline does not address this supplementary question, even though its reputation and legitimacy rest on the claim that its knowledge is guaranteed by scientific method. Recently, this was brought home to me when I attended a select meeting organized and financed by the British Psychological Society. Top British psychologists (mostly Professors) gathered for a weekend to do some soul-searching about the state of British psychology and to consider its future. To the often-asked question, 'Wherein lies our particular strength?' (frequently asked in a marketing context),the answer was usually, 'in our scientific methodology'. The idea was that students trained in psychology were of use in an almost infinite number of (employable) situations because of their knowledge of scientific (read quantitative) methods.

There is an inscription on the façade of the Social Sciences Research building at the University of Chicago which reads 'IF YOU CANNOT MEASURE, YOUR KNOWLEDGE IS MEAGER AND UNSATISFACTORY'. The philosopher of science who notes this goes on to comment that those who are working inside its laboratories 'scrutinize the world through the iron bars of the integers, failing to realize that the method they endeavour to follow is not only necessarily barren and unfruitful, but also is not the method to which the success of physics is to be attributed' (Chalmers, 1976, p. xiv).

Despite 20 years of involvement with psychology, the dogma of measurement still has the capacity to astound me, for two reasons. First, that I cannot understand how psychologists believe that with these methods they will understand people. If the rejoinder to this is 'But that's not what psychologists are employed to do', it makes my question all the more urgent: well what do psychologists do? Canguilhem, a philosopher of science, has argued that since behavioural psychology cut itself off from philosophy, debarring it from asking 'What is psychology?', the question that must be posed instead becomes 'What do psychologists expect to achieve in doing what they do? In the name of what have they set themselves up as psychologists?' (1975, p. 380). Second, very few psychologists have any idea of the debate about the status of science and social science and the well-established critiques of the idea of science as progress towards truth. If the method is central to the legitimacy and usefulness of psychology, one would expect that part of psychology's core curriculum would be an examination of the history and foundation of those methods. History courses, where they do exist, tend to recite the history of psychology as progress towards truth, thus reproducing the belief rather than examining it. What accounts for this widespread omission of a critical history and philosophy of psychological method? It cannot be a mistake. What practices, subjectivities and discourses reproduce it?

Biology and a Materialist Psychology

It was the spectacular developments in biology which provided the conditions for psychology to escape its roots in philosophy and theology and to claim the status of science. By naturalizing the mind, psychology provided a bridge between biology and the social sciences. The unitary rational subject of Western thought pre-existed developments in biology, which modified rather than transformed it. Basically, behaviourism was the culmination, for psychology, of the dominant positivist, anti-innatist proposition that all viable knowledge must have an experiential foundation in sensorily apprehended reality (see Giddens, 1974, pp. 3–4).

For early 'faculty psychology', the legacy of religion-based philosophy, 'experience was regarded as a function or activity of the soul, or of a part of the soul distinguished as the mind; or "the mind" was synonymous with "soul"' (McDougall, 1923, p. 13). Ideas psychology, in contrast, emerged at the time when '"ideas" were brought into the mind and changed their character. John Locke . . . began by defining "an idea" as anything whatsoever of which a man thinks' (McDougall, 1923, pp. 13–14). McDougall continues by showing how this view came to be based in biology to produce behaviourism: 'Experience became a mere stream of "ideas" and the course of experience was to be explained by the action of "ideas" upon one another' (1923, p. 14). The answer to the question, 'What are ideas composed of?' was 'sensory elements' and through this recourse to physiology, 'ideas' were naturalized. One further development was crucial:

> The full persuasiveness of this translation of psychology into terms of brain-mechanism is only to be understood when it is realized that, in addition to providing what seemed an equivalent in the brain for every sensation and a plausible scheme of the way in which these brain-elements might be supposed to play on one another, physiology was working out at the same time a scheme which claims to be able to explain, in principle, all human action in terms of the mechanics of the nervous system. This scheme is a development of the principle of *reflex action*. (McDougall, 1923, p. 22)

In McDougall's time the principle was more commonly formulated as: 'every human action is a mechanical response to a stimulus' (1923, p. 24). This early behaviourism was adhered to by 'a majority of academic psychologists of the present day' (p. 27). For them 'the nervous system has taken the place of the soul, or mind, or self, or the subject of experience' (p. 27). Ideas of mind, self and subjective experience have remained outside mainstream psychology ever since, in its efforts to ally itself with natural science and not philosophy.[1]

In 1919, J.B. Watson, the first American popularizer of psychology wrote *Psychology from the Standpoint of a Behaviorist*, a book whose basic message was that society and business should apply psychology so that it could more effectively control people. In one of the most recent compendiums of applied psychology, Watson's message is summed up as:

> Watson believed that social control was the major result of applying psychology. Psychologists had to go beyond merely predicting behaviour; they had to formulate laws to enable society to control that behaviour. In effect the psychologist was replacing the clergyman and the politician in the maintenance of social order. Behaviourism would replace the trial and error methods of the political process with the new and efficient scientifically-based technology. (Goldstein and Krasner, 1987, p. 3)

Fifty years after Watson, another American psychologist expressed the imperialistic aspirations of the latest application of behaviourism, operant conditioning. In 2001:

> the behavior shapers would be 'everywhere', the target behaviors 'all kinds', the environments invoked would be 'everywhere' and the behavioral products would be a 'happy, productive culture without war, poverty or pollution'. (Goodall, 1972, quoted in Goldstein and Krasner, 1987, p. 241)

Unbelievably, Goldstein and Krasner comment: 'in the hope that we are at least substantially moving in that direction' (1987, p. 241). Yet they have just summarized the story of Watson, highlighting his great achievements in selling on behalf of American corporations. We learn that for Johnson and Johnson, baby powder was advertised so that it would invoke the fear response in mothers, and that Watson first recommended that shops place sweets near the payout to increase sales. In the next breath (without commenting on the contrast) Goldstein and Krasner quote Watson's belief in 'applying psychology for better living, health, happiness, wealth [whose?], sexual satisfaction and all the good things in life' (1987, p. 2). The values are starkly those of possessive individualism and it is clear that they are on behalf of capitalism when we learn that Watson was quite explicit that his method of child-rearing had the aim of 'producing disciplined and well-behaved workers for American industry' (Grimshaw, 1986, pp. 244–5).

To Canguilhem's question with which we started, the answer must be given, 'Psychologists set themselves up in the name of science to achieve control – over others.' This is not to prejudge the question of when and how that control may be against the interests of those subjected to it: we must remember that most psychologists see themselves as promoting human welfare.

McDougall was passionately opposed to 'atomistic psychology' as he termed it. His plea to the student presented with the dominant behaviourism is worth reproducing, because it has the freshness of someone who is still in touch with what psychology might have become:

> Some, and I hope this book will increase their number, will hesitate (to accept behaviourist explanations), remembering vividly perhaps some devastating conflict of desires, some moral struggle hardly won, some intense pain, some base temptation, some impulse of profound pity or of tender devotion, of fierce anger or horrible fear. They may ask themselves: Is there not something radically wrong with a system of thought which tells us that these experiences are of no account in the world? Must there not be some flaw, some ill-founded premise or assumption, in the argument which leads to this incredible conclusion? (McDougall, 1923, p. 27)

So far I have been discussing the foundations of laboratory psychology whose early aims were knowledge of the 'general mind'. It is also necessary to survey a different sphere of biology and of applied psychology. Psychometrics rested on developments linked with Darwinian biology, rather than physiology, and the spectacular growth and popularization of psychology after the First World War rested largely on applications of psychometrics and its conceptual counterpart, the psychology of individual differences.

Psychometrics

If it had not been for the new psychometric science based on the measurement of individual differences, the applied psychologies could not have existed in anything like the form in which we know them today. Psychometrics, the measurement of individual differences, was based on different principles from experimental psychology and it was a product of application from the very start. Cronbach, a psychometrician who had stringent criticisms of both psychologies over 30 years ago, said that correlational psychology (the psychology of individual differences) 'accepts the institution, its "treatment", its criterion and finds men to fit the institution's needs' (Cronbach, 1957, p. 679).

The importance of the new psychology of individual differences was recognized by all those involved, as can be seen from Munsterberg's claim that 'a complete change can be traced in our science' (1913, p. 10) and Burt's assertion of a 'new, advanced and separate branch' which he called 'individual differences in mind' (1924,

p. 67). In industrial psychology, for example, managerial concern with control over workers' performance made a psychology of general laws inappropriate and psychometrics came rapidly to dominate industrial psychology. As Viteles remarks:

> Industrial psychology is interested in the individual – in his reactions in a specific situation. The growth of industrial psychology has been associated with the development of psychology interested not in general tendencies, but in the problems of a single individual and in the nature and extent of his response from the reactions of other individuals. (1933, p. 29)

Two examples, the armed forces and job recruitment, demonstrate just how influential the theme of efficiency was in the growing role of psychometrics as the centrepiece of applied psychology. The First World War established the role of psychological measurement in the placement of masses of workers in standardized jobs. In the USA testing was being pioneered before the war but in 1917 when the US entered the war, the scale of activities changed. The army's Committee for Psychology was established for placing recruits and used tests for identifying a range from subnormals to officer material, eventually testing 1 726 966 men (Goldstein and Krasner, 1987, p. 109). In consequence, 'applied psychology achieved much favourable publicity, massive development funds and full respectability' (M. Rose, 1985, p. 92). In 1922 the *New York Times* reported the financial benefits of psychological measurement for job recruitment:

> Some of the backers of the Psychological Corporation believe that it would be possible to increase by $70,000,000,000 the national wealth each year by properly fitting every man, woman and child to the kind of work each could best perform. (*Journal of the National Institute of Industrial Psychology*, 1922, p. 76)

The idea of measuring the fit of workers to the new categories of industrial jobs was only possible with the discourses of natural abilities and individual differences and the technology of mental measurement. It represents an application by psychologists of Social Darwinism, which saw a genetic link between the various manifestations of unfitness and linked these to efficiency or economic utility (see Hollway, in preparation; Muscio, 1974). Nikolas Rose characterizes the differences between the two psychologies as follows:

> From Gustav Fechner's psychophysics to Edward Titchener's textbook of experimental psychology, psychological measurement operated upon the model of the experiment. It concerned a space bounded by the stimulus,

the sensation and the reaction; its object was the formulation of the general laws of experience. To be adequate to the task it was now set, measurement would have to leave the closed space of the body and the artificial territory of the laboratory. It would have to relinquish the quest for indexical measures in search of distributional rankings. It would have to concern itself not with the laws of the relation between body and soul but with the classifications of the behaviours and abilities of individuals in respect to social norms. And it would have as its object not the formulation of general laws of consciousness, of that which is common to all humans, but differences amongst individuals within a population. Only then would a psychology of measurement be able to establish itself in the space which had opened up for it in the apparatus of social administration. (N. Rose, 1985, pp. 113–14)

Experimental psychology was singularly ill-equipped to provide practical understanding about individual differences. Cronbach explains why:

Individual differences have been an annoyance, rather than a challenge, to the experimenter. His goal is to control behaviour, and variation within treatments is proof that he has not succeeded. Individual variation is cast into that outer darkness known as 'error variance'. For reasons both statistical and philosophical, error variance is to be reduced by any possible device. (1957, p. 674)

Statistics and Mass Categorization

It was the norm which allowed the formulation of the laws of this variation and hence the organization of all features of human ability within a single conceptual space. For the relationship between average and deviation was the foundation of the theory of normal distribution and the basis of the power of the normal curve. (N. Rose, 1985, p. 123)

The concept of normal underwent a massive transformation as a result of its production within statistics and its new importance to administration. The psychology of individual differences, based on the principles of the normal curve, represented a technical development with social effects:

The whole project of individual psychology depended upon . . . a congruity between norms of healthy mental functioning, norms of social demand and expectation, and statistical norms of the distribution of variations in a population. (N. Rose, 1985, p. 218)

The congruity between the last two is illustrated in the way that Burt emphasizes the coincidence between the results of mental tests on the one hand and school and work achievement on the other. Mental measurement thus serves to legitimate (and make more efficient) the social administration which was already taking place: it was now based on 'proof' of innate differences in ability. Special abilities turn out to mirror the criteria of school performance and tests for school leavers define vocation in terms of those skills required for factory jobs (Burt, 1924, pp. 72–3).

The fact that children were already brought together under the care of the authorities for the purposes of schooling, made them an accessible population to measure. It is not a coincidence that Burt's list of the branches of applied psychology (Burt, 1924, p. 67) had as their object groups who were accessible through institutions (barracks, factory, school, prison, asylum) which required methods for distinguishing potential inmates from the rest of the population. The areas of applied psychology and the institutions took as their object a group within the population which posed an administrative problem for efficiency.

Measurement and the Subject

The potential effects of psychometrics were not just economic and administrative. Now anyone could be told – on the basis of scientific evidence speedily collected – who they were (in relation to specific domains). Foucault used the concept of 'subjectification' to refer to such effects on subjectivity: in French, *assujetissement* means both the production of the subject and subjecting someone to something. Before this the subject was produced within the moral realm and was formalized in religious discourses and practices. Now the categories reflected the requirements of the institutions to which people were subject: school, armed forces, the factory, the asylum. The power of the categories lay in their ability to have material effects on people's lives, for example, the difference between a job or not. And these effects were all the more profound because of the built-in comparison of any individual with all the others in a given population. Surely this must have given a new twist to the notion of the individual – a new force to individualism. Something complex, multiple, dynamic and situational could come to be fixed by a quantitative definition of intelligence, produced according to entirely administrative interests, and have the power, through scientific comparison with others, to define people's chances and worth.

Human Relations

Human relations has a rather peculiar relation to psychology. It had never been defined as 'pure' psychology because of its critique of psychology's adherence to a natural science model. However, the conditions for what on the face of it appears to be a superior moral stance are contradictory. Human relations has been enormously influential, particularly in applied and social psychology, and this has come about because of its successes in regulating behaviour where behaviourism and measurement were either only partly successful or counterproductive (see below). It is important to situate human relations and to examine its effects because it underpins the assumptions of much feminist and progressive social psychology.

Like many psychologists emerging from higher education in the 1970s, my criticism of psychology was enabled by the existence of a humanistic discourse. Human relations appeared a relevant, personal, caring psychology which valued change and liberation. Because it shared psychology's individualist premise it was widely disseminated. Human relations derived its influence from being inserted into many areas of applied psychology (particularly clinical and organizational) and because it reflected dominant and diffuse values of the epoch: individual freedom, democracy and egalitarianism. In Chapter 2 I introduced the broader current of humanist thought and discussed human relations in this context. The main purpose of my argument there was to show up the way that human relations was trapped in the related dualisms of individual –society and agency–determinism. Maybe because it shared the same subject with orthodox psychology, its challenge was never primarily on the content of psychological theory, rather on the dehumanizing premises and effects of scientific method. Here I would like to take a more historical look at human relations and its (often unintended) effects. A rather crude summary of my argument is as follows: speaking out (or, in research terms, giving an account of oneself) is seen as the discovery of a true inner-self through the human-relations discourse and practices. This inner-self first emerged in response to the failure of more behaviouristic attempts at changing people's work-place conduct. In this model, individual change is seen as resulting from the real inner-self, not subject to external influences, and thus is the free choice of the individual. Its political and social effects are thus masked. Methodologically the meaning of a person's account is seen as a transparent reflection of experience.

Elsewhere I have charted in detail the conditions which led to the take-up and development of human relations in managing organizations (Hollway, in preparation). In the mid-1920s, employees at the Hawthorne plant of Western Electric (Chicago, USA) were interviewed in a non-directive way (later formalized as the 'counseling program') in order to get information about what was troubling them and with the intention of rendering this harmless before it resulted in loss of production. The counselling programme derived many of its assumptions from psychoanalytic principles which were influential in the early formation of human relations ideas. The need for a new method of information gathering (later met by attitude surveys; see Baritz, 1960) resulted from the immense growth of organizations and the use of a hierarchy of supervisors to control repetitive fragmented jobs so that management lost direct contact with the shop floor. Western Electric discovered how serious were the grievances resulting from the behaviour of supervisors, a discovery which culminated in human relations training for the supervisors to alter their coercive, arbitrary and autocratic conduct (Roethlisberger and Dickson, 1939). Training in interpersonal skills took a fairly behaviouristic form initially, in which supervisors learned things like asking, 'How's your wife?' (the precursor of the honeyed 'Have a nice day' which follows you out of every service building in the United States).

Later, human relations training focused on trying to produce change at a deeper level within individual managers ('personal growth'). This was in answer to the recognition that workers saw through 'inauthentic' posturing by their supervisors (Roethlisberger, 1954, p. 18). Often supervisors' application of basic coercive authority was not fundamentally affected and the acceptable mode of control and influence was in a state of transition as part of the emergence of new values about democracy in social relations. The transition is reflected in theory: Roethlisberger rejects a behaviourist underpinning to training for this reason, modifying the theory he used for human relations training so that:

> By an improvement in response on the part of an individual we shall mean an internal way of learning rather than an external technique to be learned . . . It is intrinsic to him and modifies his behaviour as well as the object or situation upon which it is to be practised. (1954, p. 169)

The objective is still to modify behaviour, but the means have become more subtle.[2] Elsewhere I conclude a discussion of these developments by asking rhetorically:

> How do you ensure change without imposing it? You convince the individuals who are the object of change that they are choosing it. This is what I mean by subjectification. Argyris calls it 'growth'. Argyris' definition of growth is telling, if seen in the context of management, or indeed any higher authority whose objectives can better be met through willing responsibility on the part of their employees, clients or patients. Growth involves '"proving" to one's self that it is one's self who is responsible for some of the problems one is facing' (Argyris, 1962, p. 156). With human relations the quest for control went to the very core of the person. (Hollway, in preparation)

Human Relations and Feminism

Since human relations treated a different theoretical object – the whole, authentic person revealed when the crap (defined in a variety of ways) was stripped away – it could oppose the objectification of people by the scientific method. This theoretical object is shared by feminism.[3]

By making language transparent – only the medium of expression for the inner truth – the forces which operate on the person to produce a certain conclusion, the discourses and practices within which they are positioned, are occluded. All sorts of control can be exercised over people in this way in the genuine belief that the values of individual choice and liberation are being enacted. I do not want to imply that the effects are always oppressive, but rather that, unless self-discovery is seen as a production, its political conditions and effects are not available to analysis. Similarly, Weedon argues that:

> The meaning of experience is perhaps the most crucial site of political struggle over meaning since it involves personal, psychic and emotional investment on the part of the individual. . . . It affects both where and how the individual acts and whether her action is based on a consensual acceptance of the meaning and effects of an action, on conscious resistance to them, or on the demands of other external necessities. (1987, pp. 79–80)

If these principles are applied to women's consciousness-raising, which had its origins in human relations practices, the argument can be clarified. Weedon continues:

> Yet it is possible to transform the meaning of experience by bringing a different set of assumptions to bear on it. In consciousness-raising, the first major breakthrough for most women is the possibility of interpreting difficulties, problems and inadequacies not as the effect of individual personal failings, but as the result of socially produced structures which maintain a division of labour by sex, together with particular norms of masculinity or femininity, and which subordinate women to men. (1987, p. 85)

Another way of putting this is that in consciousness-raising groups, women learn to position themselves in a feminist discourse. They also learn how they have been positioned in discourses which have made them feel abnormal. Suppose a group of women who are mothers form a group to discuss their 'experience' of mothering. It is important that they see how their experience of what is normal, inadequate, etc., has been produced in a whole panoply of practices and discourses which were directed at them in the hospital, at postnatal check-ups, by the health worker and in books.[4] A first step for a mother who feels deviant and inadequate may well be to discover that other mothers do not conform to the experts' norm, but it would be even more effective politically to recognize the effects of those discourses on experience and subjectivity. When 'experience' is inserted in psychological discourses, it cannot do this.

Social Psychology and Dualism

Social psychology was shaped by the dominance of Social Darwinism at the beginning of the twentieth century. While its adherence to the methods of the natural sciences hark back to the experimental psychology which was already established (see above), its questions were framed in relation to the dominant belief in the inherited basis of character and conduct: what part did society play in how someone turned out? In emphasizing that part, social psychology was progressive in the context of innatism because, unlike biology, the environment could be changed.

I am not going to treat social psychology in the same terms as the other three psychologies for the purposes of the following discussion. Social psychology shares some of the assumptions of each of the other three, and it will become particularly apparent how much it shares with human relations (in the theoretical realm, not as regards method). Social psychology is, first and foremost, the sub-discipline whose job it is to provide a way of understanding the social aspects of the individual, and this is the root of its problem, the problem of individual–society dualism (see Chapter 2). Social psychology's attempt to understand the difference between the sexes has been confounded by the consequences of this dualism. Since feminist psychology has depended on social psychology, along with human relations, for its approach to women and gender, this is of considerable importance. Therefore, I concentrate this section on the recent feminist psychology, drawing for some of my examples on *Feminism and Social Psychology* edited by Sue Wilkinson (1986), which is representative of British work in the field. Wilkinson points out (1986, p. 12) that feminists have been short on providing detailed accounts of what feminist social-psychological theory would look like. I think this is because it will have to depart so radically from its origins, and that is what I have illustrated in this book. When I was searching for a feminist social psychology to provide the ground on which I could base my Ph.D. research, what I found was work on androgyny, on sex-role stereotyping and socialization. It is the limitations of these, as they are still influencing feminist psychology, that I want to examine in detail.

Androgyny

Feminism in the 1960s claimed equality on the basis of women's sameness to men and the dominant social psychology concerning sex and gender at the time reflected that discourse. On these grounds of no significant differences between the sexes it was possible to contest masculinity and femininity scales which looked for and produced difference (difference which of course had been construed from the point of view of the masculine norm as superior). Sandra Bem, in her Sex Roles Inventory (BSRI), began with the premise of sameness between women and men, but then used the concepts and methods of the old m/f scales. The concepts of masculinity and femininity remained unreconstructed. Bem's orthodox measurement methods reproduced all the same sexist generalizations which had previously become enshrined in scientific knowledge through the measurement of 'sex differences'. (Her use of psychometrics testifies to the dominance of the individual differences psychology which I have discussed above.) What was new was that her scales produced high or low scorers on *m* and *f* among both women and men (unsurprising in a late hippie era among the West-coast students who formed not only her sample but her judges). Bem has since acknowledged the criticism that her work was unlikely to be feminist in its effect because it left the innatist concepts of masculinity and femininity unchanged: 'the concept of androgyny is insufficiently radical from a feminist perspective because it continues to presuppose that there is a masculine and feminine in us all' (Bem, quoted in Wetherell, 1986).

While Bem's work does not any longer represent feminist psychology – indeed it has been roundly criticized – it none the less demonstrates the serious limitations in borrowing the basic methods and concepts of the knowledge that needs to be overturned. Her presumably feminist intentions were subverted by the methods and assumptions she reproduced uncritically as a result of her training as a social psychologist (and the lay assumptions that it uncritically reproduces). She failed to raise theoretical questions about gender at all, but followed in the atheoretical, empiricist tradition of Anglo-American psychology. Meanwhile, the idea of androgyny was taken up with enthusiasm by an oncoming generation of progressive and often feminist American social psychologists. It fitted their training and their idealistic assumptions about gender (as well probably as their sense of their own identities). If social psychology had ever evolved any historical self-consciousness, the androgyny enthusiasts would have been able to recognize that the dominant student American position concerning gender was a historically specific phenomenon and that the concept of androgyny in social psychology was a product of similar conditions.

The lessons for us are the importance of conducting a thoroughgoing critique of theory and method in social psychology and of situating our own subjective experience as women (and feminists) in its historical and contemporary social perspective. It does not look as if these are the conclusions being drawn by many feminist social psychologists[5] and the reasons can be found in the fundamental assumptions of social psychology which are still constructing the feminist version. How did social psychology get into the position where significant differences between the sexes could be bracketed off in order to claim an essential androgyny? It is necessary to look at the fundamental dualism on which social psychology rests in order to answer this question.

When Gender is Purely Social

The psychology of sex differences was posed in the following dualist terms:

> The psychology of sex differences . . . is the study of whether or not women differ from men in some systematic way in their emotions, intellectual and social behaviour, in their attitudes, skills and interests and, if so, what is the basis of such differences? That is to say, can such differences in behaviour be attributed to some 'built in' factors which are a consequence of their sex? Or are they perhaps a consequence of the fact that boys and girls are treated differently from birth? (Hunt, 1974, p. i)

Social psychology's position was marked out on one side of this dualistic divide. Theoretical progress has been marked only by changing the either/or terms in which Hunt posed the question (back in 1974) to the notion of an interaction, which has been the dominant paradigm for giving an account of the relation between individual and society (as the years have gone by a 'complex interaction'). However, this change did not enhance the work which social psychological theory could do. Because of the reliance of the two terms on each other – individual and society by definition exclusive of each other and only ever interacting – the individual remains an asocial concept. Social psychology does not retheorize this individual but takes it as a starting point. Work on the self, or personality, or gender identity, likewise was conducted within this framework of assumptions.

Although sociology was also engaged in these debates (notably the nature–nurture debates of the 1960s), social psychology has commonly been seen as the discipline (or inter-discipline) whose job it is to give an account of the relation between the social world and the individual. A typical view is contained in this definition of social psychology by Levinson et al. : 'It creates a structure of theory and knowledge linking the disciplines that deal primarily with the individual and the disciplines that deal primarily with social, cultural and collective life' (1978, p. xii).

To do this it had to explain how that gap between individual and society was bridged, how the outside (society) got inside (the individual). Socialization theory is based on this problem, but its answer does not change the terms: internalization refers simply to the process of the social getting inside.[6] Because of the basic dualism of the terms of socialization theory, however much socialization is undergone, the core individual is inevitably conceptualized as possessing an essence which is asocial, that is biological. The social remains external and in effect (as I shall illustrate below) artefactual. The way that biology is rendered social is not theorized because the two things are juxtaposed and antithetical.

Bem's concept of androgyny and its weaknesses can be seen more clearly in this perspective. The psychological differences between the sexes were seen as an artefactual product of society underneath which lay an androgynous inner core. Because of the dualism, the effects of society never go to the core of the individual. Once these underlying assumptions are revealed, new light is cast on Bem's otherwise puzzling recommendation that psychologists 'should seek to overcome their preoccupation with gender difference' (Bem, 1983, quoted in Sayers, 1986, p. 26). I disagree profoundly. The way she uses the terms, and the conclusions which she is then forced to draw, are a product of dualism. Bem regards gender difference as existing only in the realm of ideas, not real because it is not part of the individual's essence. Therefore, she reasons, if social psychologists ceased to reproduce these ideas by their preoccupation with them, it would help gender difference to go away. As Sayers comments: 'hardly an easy task given the multifarious ways in which, whether we like it or not, social relations continue to be structured by sex' (Sayers, 1986, p. 26). Bem's position is fundamentally idealist: ideas are separate from material reality and originate in the mind of individuals. The political effect is to concede gender difference to the partiarchal regimes of truth which already construct it (and which have material effects). The resulting position, that gender difference is a natural product of biology, is dangerously close to the other, equally oppressive, position that psychology has taken vis-à-vis women; to render women's difference invisible through its use of the male norm as a universal.

Through theorizing ideas as somehow alien to the true nature of the individual, social psychology appears to depart from the Cartesian subject for whom ideas were the guarantee of the person (*cogito ergo sum*). We need to make another diversion into the epistemology of social psychology to see how Bem manages to place ideas about gender as outside the core person. Having acknowledged the criticisms of androgyny, Bem's account of gender is in terms of masculinity and femininity being themselves 'cognitive constructs derived from gender-based schematic processing' (Bem, 1981, p. 383, quoted in Wetherell, 1986, p. 83). She is using cognitive theory and the view of the individual as information-processor; aspects of the dominant paradigm in social psychology. It is through cognitive theory that the idea of sex-role stereotyping is produced, a concept which is central in the social-psychological account of gender.

A summary of my argument is that cognitive theory arrives at the notion of ideas being alien to the individual by a further, related dualism which reduces ideas to a process empty of content (information-processing empty of meaning). The individual is process and the content is placed outside, in society again (recently often referred to through the concept of ideology). This time the individual–society dualism does not pose biology directly as the basis of the individual but relies on a specific biological capacity – information-processing or cognition.

Cognition

Back in 1972 cognitive theory was already being seen as a solution to dualism: 'for socialization theory, cognitive theory was intended to solve the problem of the relation between individual and social' (Rosenberg and Sutton-Smith, 1972, p. 86). Cognition is now by far and away the most dominant paradigm, not only in the field of artificial intelligence (which in Britain is providing the only significant source of increased research funds for psychology) but in social psychology, where it produces theory which fails to incorporate content and, therefore, cannot theorize meaning.

The trouble with cognitive and socio-cognitive theory is that they inherit a cluster of fundamental and limiting assumptions from psychology, none of which will serve as the basis of an emancipatory theory of gender. Cognitive theory inherits from its precursor, perception theory, the idea of external events being represented internally through basically neurophysiological processes (as I have documented above). Cognitive theory was seen as a major advance over perception theory because it was no longer limited to the assumption that ideas were a direct, unmediated, internal representation of the external world, rather emphasizing the active role of cognitive mechanisms in organizing incoming information. In doing this, however, it did not modify the dualism of psychology's assumptions: cognition was in itself a pure process and separable from the content which comes from the outside. Any departure from the truth of external, material reality is seen as inherent in the mechanism, an effect of the principle of organizing into patterns a welter of incoming information. However, it is also seen as a deviation from how the information-processing mechanisms can ideally work. This inconsistency is swept under the carpet by recourse to an individual differences model (descriptive, not explanatory) which says that some people's information-processing is better than others, for example, the cognitively complex better than the cognitively simple.

When cognitive theory is pressed into service in social psychology, it still tends to adhere to notions of bias or error as an arbitrary result of information-processing capacity, for example, Tajfel's use of a socio-cognitive approach in social categorization theory and social identity theory, which is now dominant in experimental British social psychology.[7]

Stereotyping
In the concept of stereotyping, the cognitive explanation of error is extended to ideas in the social world which become a product of error. Allport called erroneous generalization 'a natural and common capacity of the human mind' (1985, p. 17) although he did find it necessary to include the factor of hostility to explain the outcome of prejudice.[8] Cognitive theory has become the mainstay of explanations of prejudice, attitudes, stereotyping and inter-group hostility. That cognition is based on organizing information is easily seen as accounting for erroneous generalization and premature judgement. Cognitive theory suggested that, since prejudice was based on premature judgement, stereotyping could be corrected by providing additional correct information. The political remedy was thus information-based re-education (in race relations practice, this meant multi-cultural education).

Similarly, the use of sex-role stereotyping in social psychology has produced the assumption that it is erroneous and therefore not 'real'. Socialization theory provides the additional emphasis that because children learned these stereotypes from the environment, change can be accomplished by correcting them, for example, in books and sex-typed toys. The idea of a role, which is also used as a bridging concept between the individual and social, likewise implies that gender identity can easily be changed, like unpeeling layers of socialization to reveal an untainted inner core. The theory suggests that all that is needed is re-education. When this does not work (and it is never enough), the conclusion is readily drawn that it must be a biological difference after all. The category of biological difference ('real' as opposed to artefactual sex differences), unmediated by the social world, is waiting in the wings to provide the explanation for the impossibility (difficulty) of change.

Both accounts are based on assumptions about universal biologically-based processes or capacities, assumptions which are incapable of actually addressing individuality. Why, according to these accounts, is sex-role socialization not successful in all cases? As a result of dualism the answer reverts to the extrinsic social factors (different environmental influence). An explanation of individuality is left, by default, to the model of individual differences, which at bottom assumes that differences are inherited. It is paradoxical, but as long as it is based on dualism, psychology cannot get a grasp on that question which is in principle its subject matter, how to understand individuality.

As long as gender is understood, through cognitive theory, as sex-role stereotyping, it will be seen as reproduced arbitrarily through error, rather than being motivated. This has powerful implications for practice. Androgyny is the other side of the coin of sex-role stereotyping. If, deep down, people were androgynous, then re-socialization – in the form of changing stereotypes, providing un-biased information and providing different models – would provide the transformation required for equality of the sexes. But this formula can also imply that if these things are not done, then 'internalization' of sex-roles is an inevitability. Sexist ideas, or ideology, are by implication monolithic.

Cathy Itzin's (1986) work on age–sex stereotypes takes this line and demonstrates the limits to which the stereotyping and socialization paradigm can be taken by feminist social psychology. She provides a powerful description of media and other public images in which sex and age stereotypes combine to provide a picture of older women as worthless. The only account available to her of how these work on actual women is internalization. Because this concept is not really a theorization of a process, just a word which is necessary to provide for the external getting inside the person, it implies by default that there is a one-to-one correspondence between media images (or other articulations of sex-role stereotypes) and women's identities. This assumption has been uncritically reproduced in the literature. For example, Margrit Eichler, whose book raised some early questions about androgyny, is satisfied to quote Money and Erhardt's tautologous definition that gender identity is the 'private experience of gender role and gender role is the public expression of gender identity' (Eichler, 1980, p. 60). The unashamed tautology can only mean that the idea of a one-to-one correspondence between word and meaning, or image and effect, is just not perceived to be a theoretical problem.

It is a problem for feminism.[9] But to escape the determinist implications of a dualistic theory of socialization that says that stereotypes produce identity, feminist social psychology has tended to resort to that other implication of the same dualism which says that stereotypes are social and therefore not the same as the essential core of identity. Itzin opts for this formulation, presumably to escape the first. She juxtaposes 'what we know is true' (the inner, asocial identity) with 'the lie about us' (1986, p. 129) and similarly 'we live both our "reality" and the "reality" of oppression'. Her use of scare quotes around reality suggest that it is not an inevitability and she goes on to suggest a dynamic and contradictory process: 'we submit to the stereotypes and resist them simultaneously' (1986, p. 129). She uses the concept of 'double consciousness' to get to a formulation which holds on to multiplicity and contradiction. But it is the double consciousness of dualism, rather like the 'I' and 'me', or individual and social self, of Mead's theory on which symbolic interactionism is based. In it the unitary nature of women's subjectivity is not trans-cended because only one self has the status of truth and reality. Where does this self come from which is resisting the stereotypes – the 'true' self? In her account it is necessarily asocial because the social is monopolized by the other self, which is not real because it is a product of (in this case) patriarchal ideology. The idea of the real self, beyond sexist ideology, appeals because it gives a name to something we experience (or at least I do). I do not want to dismiss this, whatever it is, just to retheorize it so that it will take feminist understanding further.

Women's Experience

At this point it is possible to see how human-relations and social-psychological paradigms work together to inform assumptions about gender and women's experience. Social psychology provides con-cepts to understand the social aspects of women (role, stereotype, socialization) and human relations fills in the idea of the inner core, the asocial bit. However, the picture of the relation between the two is complicated by changing feminist discourse in the last 30 years. As I have argued, androgyny and sex-role socialization were based on a politics of women's basic sameness to men. The feminist position which has largely succeeded androgyny is based on a recognition of, and celebration of, women's difference from men. Therefore, it is not going to embrace a psychology which is ignoring women's difference.

However, feminist psychologists are in a tricky position (as I demonstrate in the case of Judi Marshall below) because the notion of gender difference has not been reclaimed from its old insertion in a sexist discourse where difference ultimately finds its guarantee in biology and thence can not be changed. As Genevieve Lloyd puts it:

Unless the structural features of our concept of gender are understood, any emphasis on a supposedly distinctive style of thought or morality is liable to be caught up in a deeper, older, structure of male norms and female complementation. The affirmation of the value and importance of the 'feminine' cannot in itself be expected to shake the underlying normative structures, for ironically it will occur in a space already prepared for it by the intellectual tradition it seeks to reject. (1984, p. 105)

So, understanding gender difference does not seem to be on the agenda for feminist social psychology at the moment. Instead, the focus is on women. I believe that this is unfortunate for two reasons. First, there is a danger of taking women as a category and leaving men outside the account, because gender is produced through difference, in relations, and so if the other side of the relation is out of view, a social psychology of women's experience cannot produce a theory of how women are produced. Secondly, description without theory is not possible and accounts of women's experience cannot operate in a theoretical vacuum.

There is a danger of using women's accounts descriptively to make assertions about 'women' as a category. It is a point which is frequently rehearsed in the women's movement which is aware of the logical extension of its critique of the way that partiarchal social science has drawn universalizing conclusions which render women invisible: it would be an equivalent oppression to do the same to women who were different from the white Western middle-class norm of the women's movement. As a result, Stanley and Wise claim that women should limit their conclusions to their own cases, because it is not possible to represent faithfully the reality experienced by other people (Wilkinson, 1986, p. 17). I think this conclusion is misjudged. For a start it assumes that their accounts of themselves faithfully represent their own reality, an assumption based on the mistaken notion of some simple correspondence between past experience and present account. Even if it were possible to be purely descriptive, they forego the greatest promise of feminist research, that it can theorize about women and about gender difference. With the right theory it can do this in a way which makes carefully specified generalizations, but can stipulate their limits and not tip over into imperialistic claims about universal women's nature. Since pure description is not possible, descriptive accounts of women would be underpinned by assumptions of biological difference because there is no other viable theory available in social psychology.

The idea of women's experience seems to reduce to biology through idealism: women 'know' by virtue of being women (biological women). This effect is not at all what most feminists intend, but that is just my point. If feminist research does not go beyond the concepts of social psychology, these are the unintended effects. The feminist social psychological approach to women's experience has come about through retaining a focus on the individual, rather than relations, power and difference. It is produced by the lack of a theory of the social production of gender through meaning in the psyche, and by the avoidance of difference as a terrain because it has reproduced sexist categories of masculinity and femininity. These concepts derive their meaning from an entire discourse where a network of propositions and implications bear on that meaning and its effects. Woman and man as concepts derive their significance from their difference from each other. If there is no account of the production and reproduction of this difference, women will be seen as a product of nature.

There is in my view already evidence that this theoretical lack is undermining feminist research, whose focus is women's experience. That Bakan's (1966) dichotomy between 'agency' and 'communion' seems to have been received enthusiastically by many feminists is a case in point. The dichotomy occupies the identical theoretical space to the discredited dichotomy of masculinity/femininity, including its reliance on a biological base of difference. Judi Marshall, whose work has done much to popularize Bakan's dimension among British feminist social psychologists, resorts to anatomy as 'the least socially contaminated perspective on differences between the sexes' (1984, p. 70). This argument is a powerful example of my contention that dualism operates to leave biology without a social component. I maintain that, since the difference between male and female anatomy derives its meaning through language, it is redolent with social significance. The development of Marshall's argument unwittingly demonstrates just this point: 'male sexual characteristics of thrusting, penetration, firmness and activity have clear links to the agentic' (1984, p. 70). Notice how, for example, the meaning of 'activity' here has been completely caught in a sexist discourse of gender difference at the very moment she is purporting to describe something relatively uncontaminated by the social sphere. Marshall goes on to advocate a union of the communal and agentic styles, suggesting that women are more capable of both because 'female can be interpreted as communion and agency in unsplit wholeness' (1984, p. 72). The only justification for this claim is an unconnected reference to women's 'genital androgyny'.[10]

In effect the dimension of agency and communion reproduces the assumptions of masculinity and femininity in an androgyny paradigm. The main difference from both the old *m/f* and the androgyny paradigm is that it comes from a political position which celebrates rather than denigrates women's difference. I do not believe that this change will pull any weight when it comes to having feminist effects. I was painfully aware reading Marshall's book on women managers (1984) of the truth of the argument about language producing thought rather than vice versa. There was much that was exciting and challenging in the book, but it was squeezed inconsistently into regimes of truth which turned round its implications so that it has little radical political bearing on how discrimination in management works and how it can be changed.

There is a simple way of pointing to the inadequacy of using agency and communion (or for that matter, abstract justice versus caring and prioritizing relationships: Gilligan, 1982) to understand gender difference: how could it make sense of the phenomenon of Margaret Thatcher? The 'Thatcher factor' is a simple yardstick against which to examine how the notion of women's experience is used in feminist research. When women are agentic, take refuge in abstractions, appear incapable of empathy and revel in the use of power to undermine the rights of others, do we start to call them men? And what about the men who do not behave in these ways? These questions point to problems which require a complex theory of gender, which reduces neither to social factors nor to psycho-biological ones. In the final chapter, I apply these precepts to an understanding of how gendered subjectivity is implicated in the production of psychological science.

7

Gender, Psychology and Science

Evelyn Fox Keller points out two notable omissions in most studies of science:

> First is the failure to take serious notice not only of the fact that science has been produced by a particular subset of the human race – that is almost entirely by white middle-class men – but also of the fact that it has evolved under the formative influence of a particular ideal of masculinity. . . . Second, and related, is the fact that, in its attempts to identify extra-scientific determinants of the growth of scientific knowledge, the social studies of science have for the most part ignored the influence of those forces . . . that are at work in the individual human psyche. (1985, p. 7)

The work of Brian Easlea on sexism and the history of science (1981) remains an important exception to the first omission and Keller's own book *Reflections on Gender and Science* (1985) tackles both issues, approaching the scientific psyche from the perspective of object relations theory. In this chapter I draw on these critiques of natural science in applying the theoretical principles outlined in this book to psychology and psychologists, before finally considering what implications this has for the pursuit of a feminist psychology. Given psychology's longstanding allegiance to the natural sciences, it is not surprising that the parallels between Easlea's work on physics and Keller's on biology on the one hand, and psychology on the other are so marked. However, the fact that the object of psychological science is not nature but people raises some further questions about how the division between subject and object (scientist and 'subject') is continually reproduced, and how objectivity is implicated.

No one would deny that science has been produced by men and a particular subgroup of men at that. Many would deny that this fact has had any effect on the product, asserting that the methods of science guarantee the product's immunity from influence by the beliefs and social position of the scientists. None the less, philosophers of science across the political spectrum, 'in their attempt to defend science as a rational activity . . . attach significance and importance to the aims, attitudes and decisions of individual scientists. In this respect there is a subjective element to their position' (Chalmers, 1976, p. 137). For example, Popper, who is so concerned with setting out the principles and procedures of a truly objective science, relies on the concept of 'critical rationalism', which refers to the correct scientific attitude (Chalmers, 1976, p. 138). Modern ideas of rationality and scientificity are inseparable. The concepts emerged interdependently within the same historical conditions, as did the modern concept of masculinity. Simmel, writing in the early twentieth century, articulated what was normally assumed when he wrote:

> The requirements of . . . correctness in practical judgements and objectivity in theoretical knowledge . . . belong as it were in their form and their claims to humanity in general, but in their actual historical configuration they are masculine throughout. Supposing that we describe these things, viewed as absolute ideas, by the single word 'objective', we then find that in the history of our race the equation objective = masculine is a valid one. (Simmel, 1923, quoted in Keller, 1985, p. 75)

Grimshaw argues that in the work of Aristotle or Plato there was no notion of femininity, 'nor of a masculinity which is essentially defined in opposition to that' (1986, p. 63). She identifies Rousseau's thought as articulating for the first time (in the mid-eighteenth century) 'the idea of contrasting or complementary psychologies of masculinity and femininity' (1986, p. 63), related to an emerging distinction between private and public life which accompanied restrictions on women's economic activity. The effect was that men (the specific subset) avoided the affective by producing it as a particularly feminine characteristic (it was not denied in black or working-class men though, whose link to nature was through their equivalence to 'animals'). The affective was expunged simultaneously from scientific, rational and male thought. 'Adherence to an objectivist epistemology, in which truth is measured by its distance from the subjective, has to be reexamined when it emerges that, by this definition, truth itself becomes genderized' (Keller, 1985, p. 87).

Male Mind and Female Nature

The way that modern science emerged was already gendered and this was a condition of the later concepts of masculinity and femininity. Francis Bacon, writing in the early seventeenth century, is commonly acknowledged as the scientist 'who first and most vividly articulated the equation between scientific knowledge and power, who identified the aims of science as the control and domination of nature' (Keller, 1985, p. 33). For Bacon the scientist is male (of course) and nature female, and this metaphor for their relationship pervades his writing (see Easlea, 1981; Keller, 1985). The 'coupling' of the two terms (as Keller calls it) varies from 'a chaste and lawful marriage between Mind and Nature' (1985, p. 36) to servitude ('I am come in very truth leading you to Nature with all her children to bind her to your service and make her your slave', p. 39), to something akin to rape ('the power to conquer and subdue her, to shake her to her foundation', p. 36).

This is all very well but scientists and rationalists will object that metaphor is sheer whimsy and has nothing to do with 'real' meaning, which is characterized by logic. In contrast, the theory of meaning that I have applied is capable of conceptualizing the suppressed significations of nature on the metaphoric axis and theorizing its effects. Moreover, the scientists' objection cannot explain how, during the seventeenth and eighteenth centuries, the conception of nature changed from an active, powerful partner (as in alchemy) to something passive, determined by mechanical laws. Prior to the seventeenth century, knowledge of nature did not involve the principle of difference from nature which dominates in modern science. Knowledge was rather seen as a joining with nature; getting close enough to understand. An account of a historical transformation, whether it is the seventeenth-century one, or the one that I would like to see take place in contemporary psychology, involves huge movements in practices and structures as well as knowledge, but the reproduction and modification of these pass through people, through their actions, understanding and commitments – and people's subjectivities are simultaneously changed by these forces.

Just as I have emphasized throughout this book, how so much of psychology's knowledge hinges on the mistaken assumption of the possibility of transparent language, Keller points out that scientists hold 'the widely shared assumption that the universe they study is directly accessible, represented by concepts shaped, not by language, but only by the demands of logic and experiment' (1985, p. 130). Scientific knowledge is a privileged form 'dissociated from other modes of knowledge which are affectively tinged and hence tainted' (p. 142). The idea of objectivity relies on this view of meaning. Easlea claims, on the contrary, 'that it is precisely through people's rhetoric, and particularly metaphors, that one can gain partial insight into motives and more importantly, unconscious motivation' (1983, p. 7). Until there is a way of theorizing how subjectivity is implicated in producing science, challenges to the principle of objectivity are on weak ground. I have argued in this book that such a theory must incorporate a theory of meaning if it is not to get trapped in dualism.

To talk about subjectivity in science is to talk about gender, since no subject is non-gendered. However, gender must mean something that is not determined, not homogeneous, not monolithic. This is the idea of gender that I shall apply in what follows. Keller's conclusions regarding the connections between mind and nature are far-reaching:

Having divided the world into two parts – the knower (mind) and the knowable (nature) – scientific ideology goes on to prescribe a very specific relation between the two. It prescribes the interactions which can consummate this union, that is, which can lead to knowledge. Not only are mind and nature assigned gender, but in characterizing scientific and objective thought as masculine, the very activity by which the knower can acquire knowledge is also genderized. The relation specified between knower and known is one of distance and separation. It is that between a subject and an object radically divided, which is to say, no worldly relation. Simply put, nature is objectified. Bacon's 'chaste and lawful marriage' is consummated through reason rather than feeling, through 'observation' rather than 'immediate' sensory experience. The modes of intercourse are defined so as to ensure emotional and physical inviolability for the subject. (1985, p. 79)

Keller is able to come to these conclusions through the use of object-relations theory (not the Kleinian but the American version, associated with the names of Fairbairn and Guntrip) to theorize the psychic forces underlying the relation of subject/scientist to object/ nature. In this theory the achievement of separation is the principal issue for the infant, separation from the original unity with the mother. Separation is not a once-for-all achievement. The infant's phantasized fear of engulfment by the mother (and also the fear of wanting it) constantly propel the child defensively to strive for separation.

The Objectification of Nature

I regard the emphasis on the distance and difference between subject and object as of paramount importance but I want to restate Keller's argument in my own terminology in order to avoid the reductionism of psychoanalysis (see below). Scientific practices are characterized by two fundamental tenets: 'the beliefs that nature is (1) objectifiable and (2) knowable' (Schrödinger, 1967, quoted in Keller, 1985, p. 141). Both of these prescribe very distinct positions for the scientist in relation to the other: subject/object, knower/ known. Consistent with my previous analysis, I want to look at scientists' subjectivity in relation to these differentiated positions, made available in scientific discourse and practice: how is the subject implicated and what differences (including gender differences) affect the scientist's relation to the position of subject? The position of scientist confers a relation to the object, which is nature as passive and mechanical; to be acted upon and controlled.

Brian Rotman, a mathematician, has come to similar conclusions about mathematics. He talks about mathematicians' relation to their subject in terms of the Lacanian concept of desire:

The desire's object is a pure timeless unchanging discourse where assertions proved stay proved forever (and must somehow always have been true), where all the questions are determinate, and all the answers totally certain. In terms of the world, the desire is for a discourse that proxies the manipulation of physical reality achieving a perfect and total control of 'things', where no realisable process falls outside mathematics' reach. (Rotman, 1980, p. 129, quoted in Walkerdine, 1988, p. 188)

Valerie Walkerdine argues that 'reason's dream' is indeed gendered: 'a fantasy of an omnipotent power over a calculable universe' (1988, p. 190). The fantasy of mathematics' total control is very relevant for a consideration of psychometrics and, more generally, the way that natural science is in the thrall of quantification. But here let me follow Keller's argument, which relies rather on nature's gender.

The fact that nature signified metaphorically as female contributed to the propensity to think of science and technology in terms of domination of something inferior. My argument, like Keller's, is that the connection between scientific objectivity (resulting from the subject–object split) and domination or control cannot be understood without reference to gender, but gender signifies metaphorically in science and is suppressed in the dominant discourse.

Psychoanalytic Reductionism
According to psychoanalysis, separation from the mother is achieved within the triangular relation of mother–father–child, and is a product of the Oedipus complex. Boys achieve it more traumatically than girls. Separation is thus inevitably gendered. Keller summarizes the implications for science as follows:

My argument, then, is that the specific kinds of aggression expressed in scientific discourse reflect not simply the absence of a felt connection to the objects one studies but also the subjective feelings many children (and some adults) experience in attempting to secure a sense of self as separate from the more immediate objects of their emotional world. . . . The need to dominate nature is, in this view, a projection of the need to dominate other human beings; it arises not so much out of empowerment as out of anxiety about impotence. (1985, p. 124)

While there is much of value in Keller's psychoanalytic argument, I believe that the use of psychoanalytic theory in a reductionist way can lead into several blind alleys. One is that a normative theory of development results, in which ego strength is in most cases gradually achieved through development and other cases are seen as pathological. For normal people there is a developmental reduction of projection and other defences. In this view, normal science could still achieve independence from unconscious forces. Second, and linked to the normative account, the reductionist use of psychoanalytic theory can lend itself to an individual-differences view, whereby some classes of individuals retain particular needs – for example, the defensive need of separation – which affect their later choices. Keller tends towards this view concerning scientists. She develops her analysis through using Shapiro's delineation of types related to the (somewhat discredited) psychosexual stages, obsessive–compulsive, neurotic, etc., and finds parallels between his description (see below) and the practices of scientists. She ends up arguing that individuals elect to be scientists because of the match between science's principles and their own proclivities – for domination, maintenance of separateness and so on (Keller, 1985, p. 124). What her account does not do is to show up subjectivity as part of a continuous cyclical reproduction and modification of forces which include structures, practices, knowledge and subjectivity. A third danger of using psychoanalysis without an intermediate theory of meaning is specifically related to its theory of gender: a consequence of gender difference being understood as achieved at the Oedipal stage is that differences between women and men then tend to get seen as fixed, with gender equated to sex (I discuss this further below).

I want to introduce a different emphasis in the idea of defensive separation. I still see it as achieved through the defence mechanisms, in which self must be differentiated from other, in order to maintain a fragile and always fearful separation. However, I do not want to reduce this separation simply to a protection against engulfment – though that may be an early dynamic – because that reduces it to process. In my subsequent analysis I distinguish the psychic objects which a position as subject in scientific discourses and practices enables the scientist to keep at arm's length, to render non-threatening, to control.

The Suppressed Significance of Woman and Nature

What is the connection between nature and woman? I do not mean nature as it is rationalistically and reductively apprehended, but nature signifying metaphorically, in which, through condensation, significations of woman are contained, though suppressed. There is a close parallel between the meaning of woman and the meaning of nature which suggests the same threat and the same defences. The signifier 'woman' contains an interesting contradiction, between subordinate and powerful, weak and threatening. Below the image of woman as weak and subordinate in dominant Western discourses is an image, often sexualized as in the image of the seductress, of terrifying power, the power to strip a man of his self-control, to awaken in him huge longing.[1] It seems to me fairly obvious that this meaning of woman is achieved through the connection with the suppressed signifier of the mother. Dominant sexist discourses, in which women are positioned as subordinate, act at a cultural level as defence mechanisms, endlessly reproduced by the anxieties and defence mechanisms of individual men. Similarly with nature. Underneath the image of nature in modern science as passive and entirely knowable is a suppressed signifier of nature as the ultimate force, capable of wreaking havoc over mind and culture. It contains intimations of something which always resists being fully known (like woman) and fully controlled (like woman) – else why the emphasis on pursuit and control?[2]

Two more parts to the analysis are necessary to restate Keller's account so that it is fully social: the first makes the connection between signification and scientific discourse and the second establishes the link with scientific practice. I shall discuss both of these in relation to gender.

I have described the way men's anxiety concerning separation would lead to the reproduction of the subject–object split and thus to 'objectivity' in science, but this does not give a complete account of how the difference is achieved between mind and nature – the difference that echoes gender difference. The subject–object split is premised on distance and in my view distance depends on difference – difference in the meanings of subject and object. I have used the Kleinian concept of splitting to explain that phenomenon whereby good and bad objects in the psyche are separated. In the case of gender identity, the 'bad' objects (the ones produced by gender-differentiated discourses as inappropriate to one's sex) can be projected on to the other of the 'opposite' sex. This account emphasizes these dynamics as they continue to reproduce difference in adult relations. The analysis can equally apply to the relations of scientist to nature. The psychodynamic argument used by Keller can be restated both in terms of the theory of meaning outlined above and the application of the concept of splitting in relation to differentiated positions in the discourse of science.

Women are in a different position in relation to the separation from the mother, since mother is not just 'other' to a woman, but also signifies in 'self', through the metaphoric connection between woman and mother. Her need to separate (and her fear of engulfment) is neither the same nor symmetrical to men's. For a man the difference between himself and the mother comes to signify (at the time of Oedipus?) as the difference between woman and man.

The difference between herself and the mother for a girl or woman cannot so signify. Here my use of Kleinian concepts, with the emphasis away from childhood and upon intersubjective defence mechanisms and differentiated positions in discourse, suggests a different direction to Keller's. For a woman, the other does not easily become the vehicle for projections of unwanted parts of the self (but see below). If for men, the other/mother then contains these projections, no wonder she is threatening, and no wonder his defences lure him into taking up differentiated positions in discourses and practices if they confer superiority or control over the other.

But this position also depletes him, because of the parts that he cannot afford to contain, which are projected onto women. The historical connections between masculinity, rationality and science mean that the position of scientist already is a product of projection of these qualities and so prescribes a position and practices which rehearse a male scientist's defences against anxiety without them even having to be activated. Keller (1985, p. 121) quotes Shapiro to describe what I see as the consequent depletion of the scientist's view:

> [For this type of scientist] attention is subject to the same kind of control as is the rest of behaviour, leading to a kind of focus so intensely sharp and restricted that it precludes peripheral vision, the fleeting impression, the hunch, the over-all feeling of an object. The consequence is loss of conviction: truth is inferred rather than experienced, the basis for judgement and decisions is sought in rules rather than feeling.

As Lacan argued, the Symbolic (what in this context I am referring to as scientific knowledge) is not the product of certainty, but 'produces certainty out of a terror; control or be controlled; master the loss' (Walkerdine, 1988, p. 200).

Differences between and among Women and Men

Now this account is only any good if it can explain several things, which I shall pose in terms of the woman scientist. It must be able to account for the fact that a woman scientist can observe the rules and procedures that derive from the principle of objectivity; that she may do science the same as a man (though she may do it differently). I should stress here that if we can clarify how it is that a woman may do science the same as a man, we also have an explanation for the differences among men in the way they do science. Any theory that implies that all men are destined to do science in a way which is determined purely by the drive to separate and control is at odds with the diversity in actuality.

Let me start by quoting Keller's conclusions about women scientists:

> The metaphor of a marriage between Mind and Nature necessarily does not look the same to (male scientists) as it does to women [scientists]. . . . In a science constructed around the naming of object (nature) as female and the parallel naming of subject (mind) as male, any scientist who happens to be a woman is confronted with an a priori contradiction in terms. This poses a critical problem of identity: any scientist who is not a man walks on a path bounded on one side by inauthenticity and on the other by subversion. Just as surely as inauthenticity is the cost woman suffers by joining men in a misogynistic joke, so it is equally the cost suffered by a woman who identifies with an image of the scientist modeled on the patriarchal husband. (1985, p. 174)

In this argument, because Keller is not using a concept of meaning which understands the links between metaphor and subjectivity, which handles the multiplicity of meanings and recognizes the relation of those suppressed to those expressed, for her the contradiction is an absolute one – between two opposing unities – creating an identity crisis. The woman scientist can only choose between inauthenticity and subversion. The concept of inauthenticity, however much we recognize it from our own experience,[4] cannot help but appeal to a 'real self' (who is the woman) which leaves scientist as the role. The explanation is caught in the dualism that I criticized in Chapter 6.

A further conceptual distinction will enable me to escape Keller's conclusions (while profiting from the insights in her analysis): it is the distinction between the meanings (and practices) suggested by a particular position in discourse and the person, whose making of meaning embraces a whole sedimented history of positions in multiple discourses, positions which are often contradictory. Keller's conclusions about women scientists founder in the conflation of these two ideas or, more precisely, in the use of terminology – such as ideology and individuals – which hampers the distinction being made.

Keller is assuming that the woman scientist's self is mirrored in the object of science. My understanding of metaphor (following semiotic theory which I described in Chapter 4) makes distinctions between the signifier and signified as different aspects of signification. 'Woman' is signified in the concept of nature contained in the discourse of science but it is not identical with the signifier 'nature'. More importantly, 'woman' signified in the discourse cannot be equated with any actual woman.[5] The subjectivity of any specific woman is a product of positions in a potentially infinite number of discourses and related practices, many of which confer meanings very different to 'woman' as it is signified in scientific discourse. These meanings all have historical links through metaphoric chains which interconnect; 'signifier replaces signifier, creating complex chains in the move from one discourse to another' (Walkerdine, 1988, p. 191). In summary, although these meanings are connected, they do not make up a coherent unitary whole.

Not all of the positions that women occupy are determined by gender. The very significant difference, to my mind, between women's and men's relation to gender is that women can identify with and take up positions which are defined in relation to '(hu)mankind'. When men take up these positions, they are a repeat of masculine positions, but for women they offer quite different meanings and access to different practices. Historically, women's demand for equality was in terms of the 'rights of man' (for discussion of the example of Mary Wollstonecraft, see Grimshaw, 1986, pp. 9–11) where 'man' referred to humankind. Of course this concept held the obvious masculine meanings – rationality, self-control – and was therefore contradictory with femininity, but by this route women claimed access to these characteristics for themselves.

One of the reasons I have made this conceptual distinction between women's and men's relation to gender, and why I see it operating, is that I recognize it in my own experience. I analysed it in my thesis (1982, ch. 8, under my pseudonym). In *Changing the Subject* I referred to it as follows:

> Early modern feminism was telling women like me that we were equal to men because we were the same as them. Certainly this fitted in with my pre-feminist assumptions that men represented all that was interesting, admirable, powerful and desirable. I was attracted to men, partly because I aspired to being like them. I was keen to develop so-called masculine skills. . . . Why was this a problem? Surely equality was desirable? To compete with men like this necessitated a negative definition of myself as woman, and it reproduced the signifier 'woman' unchanged. Women were a group I put myself outside of. When I made generalizations about women (almost always derogatory), I did not include myself in the group I was talking about. (Hollway, 1984a, p. 229)

When science is seen as the pinnacle of (hu)mankind's achievement, women can claim access to it in just the same way that Wollstonecraft, for example, claimed the 'rights of man' (of course when women began to do so, they were bitterly opposed; see, for example, Sayers, 1983). The implication of this argument for an understanding of women scientists is that there is not necessarily a critical contradiction – nor one of which she would necessarily be conscious – between being a woman and being a scientist. There *are* many contradictions among the infinity of meanings secreted by women's multiple positions in discourses, their objects and the metaphoric meanings which are contained in them. That is what I mean by the non-unitary, non-rational subject.

This variability among people and the sedimented history which makes up their subjectivity is how I approach the question of individual differences. In this context it provides an account of differences among men scientists, among women scientists, and of similarities between men and women scientists. Differences among men scientists and among women scientists are explained by the fact that both occupy positions in widely differing discourses as well as scientific discourses and, for each scientist, chains of suppressed signification make the meaning of science unique to them. Put another way, one's relation to 'scientist' (which is the subject position in discourses and practices of science) depends on one's own psyche for its metaphoric axis. These meanings are not forever fixed by history though: new discourses and practices, making available new positions and new identifications, can establish new chains of metaphoric signification. The argument that everyone's relation to science is in some sense unique does not contradict my former argument that there is something generic to women (because of the link between the signifiers woman, mother and nature) which makes their psychic relation to the (same) position of scientist different from men's. Like me in the above example, a woman may successfully deny it, but this denial will have effects, though not necessarily in her practice of science.

There is one final piece to this argument; the one that takes into account how scientific *practice* is a product of a history in which science has developed in tandem – as simultaneous cause and effect – with a certain subjectivity characteristic of that subset of white men who have always been the scientists. The Baconian version of science gradually became dominant over others (see Easlea, 1983, for a fascinating account).[6] The more dominant the discourse, the more its rules of objective procedures prescribe the practice of scientists. But there is not a one-to-one correspondence between scientific practices and the psyche of the practising scientists. This is because science does not signify only through scientific discourses, which exist independently of any one scientist and which prescribe (in the case of science very formally) rules and procedures. It also signifies through the chain of suppressed signifiers unique to the person who is the scientist. I have called this the metaphoric axis. Scientific discourse, like the metonymic axis, appears shorn of these suppressed signifiers, with the effect that the object is made safe.[7] That people have a different subject relation to the discourse and practice of science may not discernibly affect how they do science. But if we refer back to the psychodynamic underpinnings of the relations, it is likely that those for whom the position of scientist affords protection against anxiety will be defensively attached to that discourse and practice. They will be the ones who resist doing it any other way. It is their production and reproduction of the discourse which has been the historical vehicle for science to become what it is.

Identifying with Nature

Keller cites two natural scientists whose positions are different from the subject–object separation which, she argues, characterizes science. (They are both women, but I find it hard to believe that examples from men could not be found.) Their practice is defined by joining with nature. June Goodfield says, 'if you really want to understand about a tumor, you've got to *be* a tumor' (1981, p. 213). Barbara McClintock, a cyto-geneticist, talks of 'a feeling for the organism' (Keller, 1985, p. 161). Keller has made a detailed study (1983) of McClintock's unorthodox positon in relation to scientific discourses and their effects. McClintock's work was recognized in an ambivalent way: her genius was acknowledged but marginalized. Her work did not dove-tail with the dominant concepts of her field. According to my approach, this would not just be because her theories were unfamiliar, not just because scientists were defensive, but because her meanings, on the metaphoric axis, did not coincide with those of other scientists, for example with their use of the 'master molecule' concept.

Many scientists (largely, but not solely, men) could identify with a master molecule. McClintock's identifications were different. Of her work with chromosomes she says:

> I wasn't outside, I was down there. I was part of the system. It surprised me because I actually felt as if I was right down there and these were my friends. As you look at these things, they become part of you. And you forget yourself. (Keller, 1985, p. 165)

Maybe this identification was accomplished through the metaphoric chain: scientist (woman)→(woman)→(nature) molecule. This particular chain – there could be others – is unavailable to men.

Yet it is possible to imagine a woman scientist who denies the woman part because of the felt contradiction, and also because of how it is derogated. Like men, she could project 'woman' on to nature and in this case there will be an interest in separating bad objects – still to do with woman. Reproducing the subject–object split in scientific discourse would accomplish that identification with scientist against nature (woman). Her interest in doing this should not be construed as pathological, for example as her need to deny her 'femininity'. Simply by virtue of training to be a scientist, repro-duction of the scientist–nature split will be achieved; it will position the scientist and direct her/his practice, rather than the scientist producing it (the scientist reproduces it). However, scientists' rela-tion to the object, while practising their science, will differ depending on whether they are a woman or a man. It will differ because of their other positions and practices, in other discourses. These may ostensibly be quite separate, as is consistent with a view of multiple positions in discourses. However, they are never completely separ-ate, not because of an essential unity of self, but because of the chains of metaphoric meaning which insist upon connections, unconsciously if not consciously, as in my example of woman and nature.

In order to explain a man scientist's possibility of not being fully positioned in the dominant scientific discourses and practices, it must be remembered that science is not unitary; there are metaphoric chains of meaning through which a man can identify with nature and these are not all captured by the dominant science, or indeed by science at all.[8] While I am not in a position to analyse these in natural science, I have already sketched that diversity in psychology.

Psychology and the Subject–Object Split

Does psychology achieve the same subject–object split as natural science, and if so, how? I shall discuss separately the three man-ifestations of psychology that I distinguished in Chapter 6, before finally considering the conditions for the success of feminist psychology's intention to avoid the subject–object split.

Keller (1985, p. 124) claims that the need to dominate nature is a projection of the need to dominate other human beings. By this token, psychology would be the science where this need could be enacted more directly. But my historical analysis implied that orthodox psychology reduced mind to nature, which suggests that it is involved in a double distancing: on to nature and through that back to people. A further complication when considering psychology, is that the unitary rational subject – which I have argued is par excellence the subject of science – is also the theoretical object of psychology. This inconsistency is not difficult to appreciate historically: before its naturalization, mind was the theoretical object of Western philosophy, which treated it as the expression of the unitary rational subject (see Venn, 1984). As I showed in my brief history, it was this understanding of mind which was captured by natural science. None the less, in the practice of experimental psychology, it seems to me that a split occurs between mind and nature which echoes that indicated by Keller.

The procedures of experimental psychology virtually impose distance: the subject matter is defined in terms (ideally physiological) which permit the separation of a particular area of performance from the person. If the researcher is present at all (it is quite likely that the technicalities of the actual experiment are left to a laboratory assistant who obeys instructions), s/he will have a standardized relation to the person being experimented upon, mediated by the principles and procedures of objectivity. Moreover, the experimentee will usually not be asked for any account of his/her performance.

Despite the fact that experimental psychology has been most interested in the mind (perception, cognition, learning, attention and memory), it has defined these in physiological terms and set up experiments which deal exclusively with performance (or behaviour). Yet on the other side of the experiment the psychologist is engaged in just the sorts of activities that would be associated with mind when it is not reduced to physiology (accounts of events or experience, questioning, giving answers, argumentation – in a phrase, making sense). Such manifestations of mind in the experimental 'subject' are bypassed and in effect suppressed. After Darwin, when 'the mind is finally reduced to the same material status as the rest of the body' (Venn, 1984, p. 135), psychologists and other scientists exclude themselves from the status of objects of enquiry (predictably, introspectionism becomes discredited). While the scientist–psychologist retains reason or mind in the full sense, the mind which is the object of psychology is reduced in the process of psychology's allegiance to natural science. Behaviourism's claim that there was nothing intervening between stimulus and response amounts to a total denial of an identity between the scientist (who retains her/his mind in between stimulus and response) and the person being researched. This is why, in McDougall's words (quoted in Chapter 6), behaviourists could reach their 'incredible conclusion'.[9]

In this light, experimental psychology may look like sheer hypocrisy, but from a position as scientist it is necessary objectivity. We cannot just say that normally well-meaning people concurred in the rules. This is an ahistorical explanation which does not ask how these principles and practices came to dominate others. Science as we know it could only become dominant because it was preferred. My argument is that it was preferred not only because of the real power it afforded, through the prediction and control of nature/people, but because it promised to meet unconscious needs for control and the protection of certainty. My understanding of this preference is that the need for certainty is primary and that control is the way to attempt certainty.

In the case of experimental psychologists, the mechanistic, stimulus–response view is that human beings must contain parts of themselves, the parts that are associated with the body and with lower animals, which are split off from their own position of scientific rationality. The Other of rationality here is not the irrational as contained in woman, but behaviour driven by forces which have nothing to do with mind, which are at the mercy of the stimulus. The split is reminiscent of the dualism of agency and determinism. The scientist remains an agent while the theoretical object of behaviourist psychology manifests the characteristics of passivity, lack of choice, reason or insight, which are anxiety-provoking and unacceptable to the rational agent–subject. No wonder psychological science kept this object at a distance. The puzzle is more why there was an attraction to having a relation with this object at all.

The simple answer is that, without a continuing relationship, the difference and distance between subject and object cannot be re-hearsed and reproduced. Freud used an example which con-ceptualizes the unconscious dynamics in operation in terms of identification and the defence mechanisms: a woman agoraphobic identifies unconsciously with a street walker. Since this is threatening (the sexuality of the street walker is not only attractive but tabooed in herself) her symptom – her agoraphobia – works as a defence against the unconscious identification (cited in Laplanche and Pontalis, 1973, p. 206). The psychologist identifies unconsciously with the position of the person experimented upon. It is threatening (and attractive) because it represents lack of responsibility and of choice, which are taboo according to the image of rational subject in which he is caught by dint of his position as a scientist and a white man. His 'symptom' is his adherence to scientific method and discourse which guarantees him the difference from the object with which he identifies. (The same arugment can be repeated but with feminine nature as the ambivalent object of identification and defence.)

Social Distance and Psychometrics

It may be objected that all this is about experimental psychology and has no relevance to applied psychology. There, one imagines, people have to be treated in full. The simplest retort is that they are not – or at least not by psychometric psychology. For example, at Rowntree's Cocoa works in the 1920s, early industrial psychologists borrowed knowledge about skilled performance from experimental psychology and devised psychometric tests which could distinguish specific skills, for example finger dexterity and visual acuity, relevant to the fragmented jobs people were doing (Hollway, in preparation, ch. 3). Rowntree's treated its employees better than almost any other large firm in the UK and espoused the value of looking after the whole person, but psychometricians believed that the entire personality was within reach of their methods. Rowntree's also used psychometric tests for assessing the character suitability of its applicants and, according to their labour manager, it proved very satisfactory (we must not forget that these tests often work well if judged against the purposes they were created for) (Moorrees and Northcott, 1933).

In psychometrics there were factors at work which were absent from experimental psychology and which eased the separation between psychologist and testee. True, procedures were adapted from experimental psychology to guarantee the scientificity of testing, but psychometrics was further helped in producing a distant and different Other by the administrative space psychology occupied (see Chapter 6). As I have argued, psychology became one of the technologies which was involved in the regulation of problem categories of people. In this domain, difference from the norm was the criterion for administrative intervention and, with the conflation of social and statistical norms, difference between psychologist and testee relied on and reproduced social differences.

Psychometric discourse and practice is produced to support the position and beliefs of those in power, as was illustrated in Rhodesia (now Zimbabwe) in the different uses of the same psychological technology, the IQ test. Before independence, black schoolchildren were subjected to mass intelligence testing (based closely on British tests from the 1950s), in order to select the top 12 per cent who were allowed to proceed to secondary school. White schoolchildren were also tested, but only if there was an individual problem for diagnosis: a reading difficulty, a general backwardness, or indeed the suspicion of genius. Psychometrics existed in two entirely separate administrative domains, involving different procedures and different effects (the white child getting extra help, the black child being excluded from education).

Most obviously, paralleling the three branches of applied psychology, we can see psychometrics applied to the mentally ill, to problem children in schools and to problem adults at work. Behind this there are other patterns: those who fall outside the norms are most often those who deviate from those who have the power to define the norm – white, middle/ruling-class men. It is now common knowledge that women and black people are disproportionately represented among psychiatric patients; that Afro-Caribbean children are disproportionately diagnosed as educationally subnormal; that schizophrenia is a working-class and black illness (manic depression is diagnosed principally among the middle classes); that there is a high correlation between class and IQ. The effect of this knowledge is in the regulation of these groups; that is, the knowledge produces power on behalf of some categories of people to control other categories. But a condition of the production of this knowledge is that the psychologists who produce it do not successfully identify with the people whom they measure, categorize, diagnose and compare.

Social differences underpin this condition: according to all three of the systems of social difference instanced here, the white middle-class man is different – he is superior. In order for this system to work at the level of subjectivity at all, he projects his 'inferior' parts onto the other categories: onto women the weakness of emotionality and lack of autonomy; onto working-class people, the absence of self-control and perspicacity, the lack of ambition; onto black people 'animal nature' and lack of responsibility. All of these characteristics involve a lack of rationality. He cannot accept these things in himself and so he cannot respect them in others. Because his ego depends on finding others to be inferior, he cannot relate to the parts in them that he must monopolize for himself. However, since psychometric tests have been constructed within these power and psychic relations, their use rehearses these defences without actively engaging the defences of individual practitioners. For example, a psychometric test keeps what is known about another under the strictest control: only items which reproduce difference are selected and remain in the test (if an item does not discriminate between one portion of the respondents and another, it is jettisoned).

Not all psychological instruments are used on deviant groups. The assessment of managers is probably the most significant and wide-spread practice in which no major social differences exist between psychologist and respondent, subject and object. Here it is rare for only psychometric tests to be used. The rationale is that good managers are so important to the organization's efficiency and profitability that it is worth spending more money on their selection. Managerial assessment centres use as many methods as can be contrived (interview, group discussion, job simulation, tests, drinks with spouses) which take days and cost a great deal. Similarly, applied research in organizations, where social differences between subject and object may be non-existent, has come up with novel methods. For example, Peter Herriot, researching how personnel managers make graduate selection decisions, used a technique which he called 'think aloud'. Basically, as managers read through application forms, they talked into a tape-recorder about what judgements they were making and how they arrived at a decision (Herriot and Wingrove, 1984). No denial of mind here.

Clearly, applied social psychology has deviated considerably from the early orthodoxy of treating mind in terms of physiological performance. Clinical psychologists have struggled for a long time not to be restricted to using psychometric instruments for the diagnosis of psychiatric patients. It is possible, though no doubt difficult, to organize and facilitate groups in a consciousness-raising mode for women, say with eating problems or depression following childbirth. Orthodoxy is not so monolithic as to exclude such practices and the contradictions within it can be exploited. None the less, psychology's methods rely overwhelmingly on quantification, and at that point the identity between subject and object is sacrificed in the desire for certainty, or control, or both in powerful combination.

Human Relations' Rejection of the Subject–Object Split
Human relations explicitly rejected both experiment and measurement on the grounds that they were dehumanizing. Thus we have a psychology which explicitly opposed the subject–object split, arguing for the identity of psychologist and person being researched. It is mainly within the terms of human relations discourse that social psychology (including feminist social psychology) has adopted different methods. (The other tradition which has had a detectable influence is social anthropology and its progeny ethnography.) In my view, this radical challenge to orthodox psychology's position in relation to its object has not proved sufficient in producing a psychology which would be emancipatory when applied in the context of feminism. A position of identification by the psychologist –subject with the person being researched is fundamental to producing alternative knowledge but, as I shall argue, it is not sufficient. One theme in the early chapters of this book was how orthodox scientific assumptions dogged my attempts to produce different knowledge about gender. My intentions, and even my capacity to identify with my research participants, were by no means enough to oppose the dominant discourse. I had access to, and positions in, alterntive discourses and practices. Yet human relations relies on an individualistic theory of change. A theory of change which reduces to individual intention will be incapable of paying any attention to the conditions in knowledge and practice which subvert good intentions.

Human relations was closely associated with the value of personal change. I have briefly shown in the history of organizational psychology how, despite values concerning the integrity of the whole person, human relations could be used to ends that were to do with regulation, that were produced out of power difference. This example demonstrated something that I believe was characteristic of human relations more widely, that individual change could ally itself with regulation just as easily as it could ally itself with emancipation. The crucial issue is the relation between the 'change agent' (a word beloved of human relations practitioners) and the person on the receiving end. Needless to say, there were many change agents who were employed by senior people in an organization in order to change others. Human relations training of managers is the most obvious example. Yet the starting principle of human relations is that someone has to choose and direct change themselves. The way that this contradiction was dealt with had the effect of concealing the power relations which existed in the group under a veil of democratic style, informality and (individual) freedom.[10] Grimshaw points out that the central idea of the person governing the theory of humanistic psychologists like Abraham Maslow and Carl Rogers was individual autonomy (at the expense of others if necessary). She argues that 'the notion of the autonomy of the self and the autonomy of individual desires is a liberal individualist one' (Grimshaw, 1986, p. 149). Early feminism was deeply influenced by these precepts (1986, p. 140ff.) and a feminist psychology could easily founder on these assumptions.

My analysis depends on theorizing the relations of knowledge and power, and the production of subjectivity within those relations. This has different implications from the understanding of personal change in human relations. Feminist psychology has placed most emphasis on method and on democratizing the relations of research, making no fundamental changes in the knowledge or theory at its disposal.[11] It stands most chance of transforming its practices in the emancipatory directions it intends if it simultaneously develops knowledge and practice and consciously modifies the structures into which these are inserted so as not to reproduce the old power relations. If knowledge and power are as inseparable as I have been arguing, these attempts will tend to produce new knowledge. However, by the same token, the uncritical use of theoretical assumptions undermines its attempts at transformation.

Identification

My analysis of gendered subjectivity and science suggests that being a woman is neither a necessary nor sufficient condition for doing psychology which is emancipatory in its effects on women. However, being a woman provides advantageous conditions for identification with the person or people participating in the research (the ones that up to this point I have been calling objects) and for distancing oneself from the circular reproduction of the status quo.[12] I am using identification in a way which is consistent with, but not the same as, its psychoanalytic meaning. Laplanche and Pontalis, whose book provides a dictionary of psychoanalytic terminology and usage, give the general definition of identification as:

a psychological process whereby the subject assimilates an aspect, property or attribute of the other and is transformed wholly or partly after the model the other provides. It is by means of a series of identifications that the personality is constituted and specified. (1973, p. 205)

The difference between the psychoanalytic concept of identification and the one used in psychology is that the former involves the unconscious. It does not assume a unitary subject because a subject's identifications are not a coherent system, but are 'diverse, conflicting and disorderly' (1973, p. 207). Like my use of the psychoanalytic concepts of splitting and projection, identification makes sense only within the framework of relations among people, or aspects of them, and thus is inconsistent with psychological definitions of the individual. Identification is not just a defence mechanism; 'not simply one psychical mechanism among others, but the operation itself whereby human subjectivity is constituted' (1973, p. 206). Therefore, it does not necessarily operate to deplete subjectivity, as in the street walker example from Freud which I used earlier. Freud distinguished a form of identification which enriches an agency of the personality, where both the identification of self with other and the other with oneself operate to create a 'we'. Applied to the scientist's relation to nature, this would result in something consistent with McClintock's description (above) of her identification with the parts of nature she was studying. No defensive differences obstruct this process.

However, to avoid being positioned by the subject–object split is not just a matter of successful positive identification. This reduces it to a notion like empathy. That split is contained and reproduced in the dominant assumptions and procedures of psychology, which, if followed, can prohibit identification or at least make it ineffective. Therefore, it is important to incorporate into each analysis the reciprocal effects between a discourse and the practices that it recommends.

My use of identification is not limited to a model of the interaction of process and practice. What is crucial, as I have argued, is to analyse the psychic mechanisms in relation to the meanings given in discourses. It is only through meanings that identifications can take place, and these meanings are not created by the individuals concerned. Women researching women can share many of the multiple meanings of woman. Their sedimented history of positions in discourses will have many common elements, as well as the differences which often produce defensive distance. Meanings are given in discourses, but they are also imbued with significance by the sedimented history (held on the metaphoric axis) of a particular person occupying the position at a given time. For example, the agency of scientist–subject in contrast with the passivity of the person–object is given in scientific discourse in the mind–nature dichotomy. One woman scientist may unconsciously identify with the passivity of the object (a part of how she has been positioned and about which she feels ambivalent) and use the subject position in the discourse of science as a defence against that identification (this parallels Freud's streetwalker example, above). Another woman may not project her own feared passivity onto nature and identify (identify with) nature's active characteristics. This outcome would produce something similar to McClintock's view of nature as a self-organizing, active system (Keller, 1985, p. 171). The effects of the two dynamics would be quite opposite; the former reproducing the dominant discourse (and in the case of women who are the object of psychology, positioning them as passive) and the latter producing emancipatory knowledge and subjectivity.

In psychology, identifying with the research 'object' requires research practices which run counter to the dominant ones, and in this the nascent feminist discourse provides support. Paula Nicolson researched into depression following childbirth by interviewing women in their own homes and contrasting the results with those of the dominant research design. These 'are relying more and more on standardized measures and "objective" data' (Nicolson, 1986, p. 135). There are structural pressures to reproduce designs which rely on questionnaires not even administered in face-to-face interview, because they can be applied with minimum expenditure of time on large numbers of women. The lack of contact between knower and known is exacerbated by the view of depressed women as 'faulty machines' (Nicolson, 1986), with the resultant failure to identify and production of women as pathological individuals. Fundamentally different knowledge is required in conjunction with such methods. If this can be achieved, all researchers, including men, are provided with positions in discourse which will not reproduce the distance and difference produced by orthodox research discourse and practice; they are provided with new channels which enable them to identify positively with the women concerned. Of course these will be opposed by many because of the defensive interest in maintaining difference.

Identification and Multiplicity

The more multiple the acknowledged parts of the person are, the more capable they will be of identifying with many different positions. I have argued that women are likely to incorporate greater multiplicity than men because of what woman means in a relation of otherness to humankind. White middle-class men are the ones who, historically, have produced the systems of social difference which have created various Others, onto which their own repressed parts can be projected. They are left with the ideal of the unitary rational subject, to which they are more or less rigidly bound by what are in effect cultural systems of defence (discourses which reproduce and are reproduced by shared defence mechanisms). In consequence, this subsection of men are most at risk of being separated from their multiplicity, from their contradictions, from their capacity to identify with others. It is this separation which results in defensive identification.

Amina Mama argues that the same principle of multiplicity applies to race:

> The capacity to occupy many social positions is true of many, if not all, black people who have lived in the West, in ways that are not necessarily so for white people who have lived in Third World countries because of the historical status of expatriate communities as colonizers. (1987, p. 367)

Mama goes on to instance how she and the black women living in Britain who participated in her research could use their similarities and differences in exploring their identities as black women:

> It is also helpful to look at how difference or distance can be harnessed in the research process . . . The fact that I was not Caribbean can be said to have enabled me to perceive the discourses from a distance. This ability to abstract from conversations in which I participated was necessary for identifying discourse as Caribbean. I was able to do the same for Black discourse, by taking up a different [Nigerian] position myself. To do research of this type it is necessary to be multiply positioned, since this is what enabled me to abstract myself enough to be able to identify discourses, yet empathize enough to recognize them and identify with participants . . . In short I have, in retrospect, exploited the fact of my own multiplicity by taking up different available positions throughout the course of this research (as Black, as a woman, as a Nigerian, as someone who has visited various parts of the Caribbean, as someone with a white English mother, as a British resident, etc.). I have played with all these similarities and differences in the course of discussions with participants. (1987, pp. 368–9)

The ability to move around between discourses and the positions they confer (the ability to 'play' with them) presupposes that unconscious forces which would prevent these parts being acknowledged are not operating. But my analysis does not reduce this problem to a matter of therapy (though therapy can effect impressive transformations in such spheres). It requires alternative discourses which produce the chains of meaning along which identifications can be accomplished.

The meanings conveyed by a discourse which does not offer one a position of identification – only of otherness – are depleted, like the production of intelligence or personality in psychometrics. If a discourse provides channels of positive identification by the meanings attaching to its positions, it makes it possible to know what someone means metaphorically, that is to identify with all the knowledge provided by connections with one's own multiple subjectivity. One can only know what another is suppressing as well as expressing by identifying with their position. Then the meaning is enriched by the metaphoric links which are conditional upon one's own subjectivity. Once these are expressed' in discourses and practices, they are no longer dependent upon a person's specific metaphoric axis.

Women, by dint of their multiplicity and otherness (to the extent that it is acknowledged with its attendant contradictions, ambivalence and loss of certainty) are potentially capable of seeing the tight reciprocity which exists between rational unitary subjectivity, the theories and methods of psychology and their effects; particularly the effects on those categories of people whom it helps to produce as different from the normality of the white, middle-class, male mind. But to do this they need to produce other discourses, which recommend other practices and other relations between researcher and participants. The same argument goes for black and Third World people (see Mama, 1987) and would apply to class difference as well. These alternatives will not be neutral nor devoid of power relations and, therefore (as feminist psychology recognizes), they need to incorporate safeguards which provide for a continuous dialogue between the researcher and the multiple meanings of the participants, so that the research incorporates their interests and objectives. There are plenty of other locations for research than the huge hierarchical institutions within which most psychological practice is defined. But it would be inconsistent with my theoretical assertion that power relations are present wherever there is the production of knowledge, if I advocated that research should not take place where there are power differences (if formal ones were avoided, informal ones would still operate). It would be a shame if, for example, the woman clinical psychologist whose example I used above was inhibited from starting a consciousness-raising group for women patients because her formal status undoubtedly gave her power in relation to the other women.

Towards a Feminist Psychology
I see the importance of a feminist psychology not primarily as a way of getting equality for women (as both subjects and objects of

psychological knowledge) but in order to provide an alternative position from which to view the psychologies that we know, which have been produced by men. My analysis of gender means that the alternatives are neither necessarily nor exclusively available to women. This means feminist psychology which goes much further than a psychology by women, of women, for women.

I do not believe that the conditions for emancipatory psychology will be achieved by women doing women's psychology in an uncritical way, reproducing the dominant psychology in an attempt to struggle for recognition and advancement within psychology's contemporary in- stitutions. Achieving a 'critical mass' of women in psychology will not make a significant difference to its effects if they are doing more or less the same psychology – albeit on women. Doing more research on women within the present paradigms could just contribute to the idea of women as the problem, the exception to the norm. Identification in the sense in which I have used it can help to prevent oppressive uses of power, but this must be combined with a thorough reworking of the discourses and practices and power relations which make up the psychology in which we are trained and employed. Then we stand a chance of our emancipatory intentions for women not being captured by existing psychology.

It is on this basis that, in the first *Newsletter of Women in Psychology*, I expressed reservations about the way that women's sections in both the British Psychological Society and the American Psychological Association define their purpose (Hollway, 1986). It is symptomatic of the dominant assumptions concerning gender in psychology (see Chapter 6) that the new British Psychological Society (BPS) section is called 'Psychology of Women', the same as the American Psychological Association (APA).[13] (The Australian and Canadian ones are called 'Women and Psychology'.)

Keller (1987, p. 80) argues that a feminist critique of science has in view the extent to which the masculinization of science 'subverted our best hopes for science'. Psychology has fallen a long way short of my best hopes by being implicated in coercive social regulation and in reproducing social differences in favour of men, white people, Western and middle-class people. In this it is not alone, but a relatively small cog in the wheel of regulatory social technologies. In one respect it bears a more central responsibility: it produces and reproduces knowledges which construct a reduced image of humanity and these knowledges not only pervade Western practices of social regulation, but position us as subjects and thus are implicated in constructing our subjectivities. When I use the term 'emancipatory', I mean a psychology which, through its practices, produces knowledge which helps women (and other subordinated groups) to emancipate themselves. Different knowledges would entail different power relations between knower and known and different practices and different subjectivities would result.

Subjectivity Reclaimed

The theory that I have developed in this book provides a whole new meaning to the term subjectivity; a term which, through its opposition to objectivity in scientific and lay discourses, has exuded derogatory connotations. The meaning of subjectivity has had distinct power implications in the sense that it has been capable of dismissing many sorts of action and account which are not based on rationality, logic and objective procedure. These forms of action and account are, for the reasons I have argued above, most likely to characterize the 'others' produced as different from white middle-class men: black and Third World people, working-class people and women.

The way I use the term reclaims it for valid and legitimate knowledge. Indeed, I claim that it provides the basis for enriched and emancipatory social and psychological knowledge. I am not just making a prescriptive or idealistic claim to accord value to the idea of subjectivity as it has signified to date. On the contrary, I have identified the theoretical conditions for subjectivity to mean something quite new and have given the example of my own research which I hope provides an indication of the kind of research practice which can result. Remember that the conclusions I draw here were a product of that research – and the theoretical work that went into it – rather than the reverse. I hope it provides psychologists with the power of an alternative discourse and practice both emancipatory and with long-term effects, within which to position their own research.

Notes

Introduction

1 An example which is likely to be particularly relevant to women Ph.D. students is Jane Selby's Ph.D. thesis whose subject is feminine identity and contradiction in women research students (1984).

Chapter 2 'isms' and 'ivity': Basic Terminology

1 I do not include psychoanalysis within psychology here. Although psychoanalytic concepts influenced parts of Anglo-American psychology up to the 1950s, its radical assumptions about the subject were excluded. Human relations psychology was heir to the sanitized remains of psychoanalytic psychology. It is outside psychology that psychoanalysis has continued to be developed.

2 Underneath this apparent reversal there lingered the therapeutic rationale that if feelings were spoken, the non-rational would be exorcised and action would be governed by rationality once again. This is certainly the argument underlying co-counselling practice. If this is the case, rationality is not displaced at all.

Chapter 4 Making Love without Contraception: Analysing Accounts

1 In one women's group I was in, a woman described going through the process of getting pregnant and then 'changing her mind' three times in one year. Sometimes it was so difficult to decide that she did not have the abortion until the fourth month. An assumption of the unitary rational subject can only 'explain' this as an aberration.

2 This extract should also raise questions about my version of what feminism pronounced as 'on' and 'not on'. My account is not an 'objective' claim about feminist discourse. Rather, 'feminism' bears the mark of my own subjective relation to it (as do all meanings in their articulation by specific people), including the meanings informed by the metaphoric axis. These meanings are, therefore, part of my relation to the feminist discourse, and historically linked to my earlier positioning in the have/hold discourse.

3 For an excellent introductory account to Lacan's theory, its importance in providing new theoretical starting points for theorizing subjectivity, and its use and criticism by feminist theorists, see Stephen Frosh's *Politics of Psychoanalysis* (1987). My account here will be limited to what is indispensable for my argument.

4 For example, Collinson and Knights (1986) have used my theorization of differentiated positions in the three discourses concerning sexuality to look at sex discrimination in the insurance sales industry.

5 All this complexity in the way that commitment signified for Jim is relevant to the initial extract in this chapter from my journal. My own desire for commitment was formed in relation to what it signified for Jim (and vice versa). He did not have to be explicit about it – suppressed significations may be read through what is expressed, both in words and actions.

Chapter 5 Relations and Subjectivity

1 It has some affinity with the phenomenon that psychology sees as cognitive dissonance.
2 In my thesis I called Will's rationalist position ('I felt quite knowledgeable about it all, there was no problem') a 'metonymic mode' (Hollway, 1982). There seemed to be a link between the rationalism which was a consequence of defences against anxiety and the sort of meaning which was achieved on the metonymic axis. This can be explained by the defence mechanisms (in Lacan's account, condensation and displacement), whereby a signifier falls to the level of the signified. What remains expressed is what is acceptable according to the precepts of the unitary rational subject. I coined the term 'metonymic mode' when, having made sense of the concepts of metaphoric and metonymic axis, I was analysing the material from Will. I still feel that there are theoretical problems with it. It is consistent with a Lacanian analysis of desire and signification, rather than a Kleinian one (which are inconsistent when it comes to their accounts of the determining influences on human subjectivity). According to Lacanian theory, that part of meaning which was pervaded by desire had fallen to the level of the signified. Using Kleinian concepts it was because of the effects of the defences mobilized in the face of his own contradiction, anxiety and lack of control.
  In either version, the metonymic mode is a consequence of the defence whose effect is to render Will out of touch with his desire to have a child, primarily because it may or may not be gratified. I realized when working on this example that it differed from the one I used in Chapter 4. There the suppressed signifier achieved signification through the metonymic axis by the process of displacement. Here Will's desire for a child is repressed (not his position of wanting one) and the defence mechanism at work appears to be projection.
3 When I use the term repression, I take it as the general term covering all the specific defence mechanisms.
4 The effect of this splitting, achieved through the relational defence mechanisms, was unitary only in relation to the characteristic that was split; in this case, giving help and being in need of help, with the suppressed signification of strength and weakness. It did not produce a simple unitary subject effect because it left contradiction as I have described above. Neither does the analysis imply that there is a splitting of a unitary subject which, if corrected, resolves back into a unitary subject. It is based on the premise of multiple and contradictory positions which are both within and between people.
5 For a clear summary, see Frosh (1987, p. 130ff.), to which my account here is indebted. Urwin (1984) has theorized Lacan's account of the Mirror phase putting power relations at the centre.
6 In this respect Klein was influenced by Fairbairn whose claim that the libido was object-seeking, rather than pleasure-seeking, represented a radical break with Freudian psychology and was the basis of the object relations school of psychoanalysis.

Chapter 6 How did Psychology come to be what it is?

1 Predictably, interest in the self has had a distinctly philosophical allegiance (e.g. Mischel, 1977).
2 At around the same time, for the same reasons, social psychology was propounding the superiority of 'democratic' over 'authoritarian' leadership styles, lending

scientific authority to what was a changing culture in power relations. It happened in the post-war climate of fear and fascism, but it was precipitated by the crisis of authority in institutions which depended on hierarchy. It was 'democratic style' that took over however, not 'democracy'.

3 Grimshaw (1986), examining the antecedents of feminist philosophy, discusses and criticizes the ideas of two of the most influential thinkers in human relations – Abraham Maslow and Carl Rogers. She points out that both Betty Friedan and Mary Daly quote approvingly Maslow's idea of self-actualization as (in Daly's case) 'exactly the sort of conception of self-realization that she wanted to see as a goal for women' (Grimshaw, 1986, p. 140).

4 Jean Grimshaw uses an example from the child psychoanalyst D.W. Winnicott, from his book *The Child, the Family and the Outside World* (1964), which illustrates the process of subjectification. She points out how Winnicott presumes to describe the feelings of the mother and addresses her as 'you', in effect telling mothers what to feel. She quotes a passage which describes how a woman is going to feel when pregnant: 'A woman's life changes in many ways when she conceives a child . . . At first it may easily happen that she resents this fact, because she can see only too clearly what a terrible interference with her "own" life it must mean . . . Experience shows, however, that a change gradually takes place in the feelings as well as in the body of the girl who has conceived . . . She slowly but surely comes to believe that the centre of the world is in her own body' (Winnicott, 1964, p. 19, quoted in Grimshaw, 1986, pp. 77–8). Winnicott exemplifies the normalizing, subjectifying power of psychoanalysis.

5 Sayers, Walkerdine and Wetherell in Wilkinson's collection are notable exceptions to this claim. They do not start from the dualistic premises of social psychology. Janet Sayers, in basing her analysis of women on the assertion that girls are taught both to expect the same as men and the opposite, (1986, p. 26), emphasizes that therefore women's identity is based upon a contradiction. Valerie Walkerdine has argued for the need to be historically and socially specific about the practices and discourses within which girls and women are inserted, and demonstrates the approach by looking at everyday social practices at school and in the family (Walkerdine, 1986). Elsewhere she has examined the way that class and gender in the post-war period worked to produce her own subjectivity (Walkerdine, 1985). Margaret Wetherell draws on a similar body of critique to argue that: 'gender is not a matter of consistent unitary single identities . . . but develops from contradictory and frequently fragmentary pieces of discourse, repertoires and accounting systems available to individuals to make sense of their position, and which historically and contingently have come to be marked as feminine or masculine responses' (Wetherell, 1986, pp. 77–8).

6 Weinreich provides a concise illustration of the various traditions from which socialization theory has borrowed in its accounts of internalization (learning theory, role theory, cognitive-developmental theory and psychoanalytic theory): 'Socialization is the means by which culture, including notions of appropriate sex-roles, is transmitted. The agents of socialization are primarily parents, teacher, peer-group and the media. There are four processes by which socialization occurs. First, skills, habits and some types of behaviour are learned as a consequence of reward and punishment. Second, parents and others provide models for roles and behaviour which children imitate. Third, the child identifies with one or both parents, a process which is more powerful than imitation through which the child incorporates and internalizes the roles and values of the parent or other significant

adult. Fourth, there is the part played by the growing individuals themselves. They actively seek to structure the world, to make sense and order of the environment. The categories available to the child for sorting out the environment play an important part in this process' (Weinreich, 1978, pp. 20–1).

7 While socio-cognitive theory has developed a long way since Tajfel's (1972) initial work, including social identity theory, these premises remain unchanged.

8 A similar critique of social psychology, but applied to the social psychology of racial prejudice and its effects in the sphere of race relations, has been made by Henriques in *Changing the Subject* (1984). For further details on Allport, Tajfel and others, see Henriques et al. (1984).

9 See Grimshaw (1986) for an excellent discussion of these and related issues.

10 This appears to draw on the work of Luce Irigaray, a French psychoanalyst and feminist. For a discussion and critique, see Frosh (1987, p. 202ff.).

Chapter 7 Gender, Psychology and Science

1 In Chapter 3 Jim exemplifies this dynamic working in one man.

2 This is a way of understanding something that otherwise I find incomprehensible: why nuclear science and technology will not own up to the fact that waste is an unsolved problem and environmental pollution is a worldwide threat. In this perspective it is that no aspect of nature is allowed to evade Man's control; technology *will* solve it and Man will prevail over Nature's disobedience in threatening to damage Mankind.

3 This struck me as particularly apposite as a description of the experimental psychological method. It is worth emphasizing that this approach is not the simple product of individual psychologists' predilections, but of what we are taught constitutes good practice in scientific psychology.

4 Evelyn Keller agrees. She comments: '[In using the term inauthenticity] I was thinking of my own experience – of what it has felt like to laugh with my colleagues at their misogynist jokes, at what it feels like to say "women, they . . ."'. She went on to point out that this is what I am getting at in using the phrase 'reproducing the signifier "woman" unchanged'. She echoes a sentiment I have expressed many times in this book when she says, 'I agree that my theoretical apparatus was not adequate to my needs' (personal communication, Feb. 1988).

5 Elizabeth Cowie's (1978) work on the signifier woman has been at pains to make the distinction between actual women and 'woman' as the sign is established in certain practices like the exchange of women.

6 I do not want to imply that the outcome is an entirely unitary science. It is worth remembering Foucault's emphasis on plurality in his historical analyses of knowledge. I do not know enough about natural science to make such distinctions here, but I have made them for psychology in Chapter 6, and I shall draw on that analysis in the following application of these principles to psychology.

7 This argument is parallel to my conclusions concerning Will and his rationalistic mode: by divesting what he said of the meanings to which it was associated on the metaphoric axis through desire, he made what he was talking about safe for himself at a conscious level.

8 Keller quotes Goodfield as saying 'We are all part of nature, and if you externalize man – which is to say yourself – you are still the victim of the Inquisition, although in a different way' (Goodfield, 1981, p. 231, quoted in Keller, 1985, p. 125). If as a scientist, whether man or woman, you could accept the parts of yourself that signify

as nature, then it would no longer feel to be an inquisition, but an exploration via what one knows of oneself, through one's subjectivity. It would be a subjective method.

9 The fact that many of the questions of experimental psychology have been extended to human beings from rats, pigeons and fruit-flies makes the treatment of experimentees as 'nature' all the easier, but it does not provide an explanation.

10 Humanistic group leaders usually genuinely believed that relationships within the group were egalitarian, and they could continue to believe this because there is no concept of power or social difference available in the human relations paradigm (we are all individuals and we are all human). My experience of these groups suggests that real democracy or egalitarianism is far from the case. The following example illustrates how social power difference (even outside the formal hierarchy of organizations) and psychic defences work together to undermine humanistic intentions.

A friend and I went along to a human relations conference where she chose an event because she wanted to explore some unresolved issues in her couple relationship, which was with another woman. The man who led the group understood what she said as the problem of her lesbianism and picked on her case. He told her to march round the room holding a cardboard roll out in front of her (like a penis). When she demurred, he insisted, on the grounds that she had to overcome her resistance in order to change. When she refused he told her to lie on the ground on her back and instructed the biggest man in the group to lie on top of her. When she fought him off, he got all five men in the group to do so and a serious struggle ensued. His actions were extreme, but not different in principle from other human relations practices. One might blame the sexism of Freudian theory, for at some level the man must have interpreted her problem as penis envy. But there remains the sadistic coerciveness of his actions (of which he was quite unaware – he saw himself as a gentle, anti-authoritarian person). I can only assume that because he was incapable of separating his own masculinity from her lesbianism, he was so threatened that he was unconsciously driven to demonstrate his (male) power over her, though he displaced the actions on to other men in the group. My purpose in telling the story is that the human relations practitioner had no access to concepts or practices which gave him insight into his own subjectivity and the power relations in which he was inevitably involved (group workers with a psychoanalytic training would have had). Moreover, the human relations discourse did construct the meaning of the situation for him, in which his own interests were opaque. It did so in two ways. First, it recommended a model of individual change which focused on feelings, not on their content. Secondly, while he was not explicitly espousing objectivity (he would have rejected the idea since it derives its meaning within the discourse of science), human relations discourse ends up producing a similar idea of neutrality. Its model of the essential individual which is beyond ideology and which can be refound by getting in touch with feelings (feelings are the unmediated expression of this inner core), lends itself to the belief in a benign neutrality untainted whether by socially produced power differences or the workings of a beleaguered psyche. The social difference – in this case a compound one of gender and sexuality – provided him with the distance which meant that he was quite incapable of identifying with my friend, for if he had done, he would have experienced first and foremost the violence that he was doing to her.

11 The concept of 'reflexivity' in Personal Construct Theory is pointing to the same idea (without a concept of the unconscious) and has been used by women

researchers to indicate the way that the researcher has something in common with the women being studied. However, it does not provide an explanation.

12 During this final chapter, as I have been trying to work out the implications of my critique for a positive practice, I have found myself using the idea of identification quite centrally in my claims. I did not know where my application of a theory of gendered subjectivity to science would lead until I got to this point. As I discussed in relation to my thesis, this uncertainty requires relinquishing a sense of control (which I do not find particularly easy), and accepting the consequent anxiety. The earlier parts of the analysis (from my thesis and in the early parts of this chapter) rely on the slightly different, though complementary, notion of projection. I decided it was better to push my analysis as far as I could take it with this emerging concept of identification. The fact that the concept does not figure earlier remains a testimony to this work not reaching a specious finality.

13 Those women involved in setting up the section had considerable difficulty in getting the section agreed at all, and they were advised that 'Psychology of Women' would be more acceptable than 'Women in Psychology' because of the political connotations of the latter (Sue Wilkinson, personal communication).

References

Adlam, D., Henriques, J., Rose, N., Salfield, A., Venn, C., and Walkerdine, V. (1977) Psychology, ideology and the human subject. *Ideology and Consciousness* 1, 5–56.

Allport, G.W. (1985) *The Nature of Prejudice*. New York: Addison Wesley. First published 1954.

Argyris, C. (1962) *Interpersonal Competence and Organizational Effectiveness*. London: Tavistock.

Atkinson, P. (1977) Research design in ethnography. Block 3, Part 5 in *Research Methods in Education and the Social Sciences* (DE 304). Milton Keynes: Open University Press.

Bakan, D. (1966) *The Duality of Human Existence*. Boston: Beacon Press.

Baritz, L. (1960) *Servants of Power*. Middletown, CT: Wesleyan University Press.

Bem, S. (1983) Gender schema theory and its implications for child development: raising gender-aschematic children in a gender-schematic society. *Signs* 8, 598–616.

Bhaskar, R. (1978) On the possibility of social scientific research and the limits of naturalism. *Journal of Theory of Social Behaviour* 8 (1), 1–28.

Bhaskar, R. (1979) *On the Possibility of Naturalism*. Brighton: Harvester.

Broverman, I., Broverman, D., Clarkson, F., Rosenkrantz, P. and Vogel, S. (1970) Sex-role stereotypes and clinical judgements of mental health. *Journal of Consulting and Clinical Psychology* 34, 1–7.

Burt, C. (1924) The mental differences between individuals. *Journal of the National Institute of Industrial Psychology* 11 (4), 67–74.

Campbell, B. (1980) A feminist sexual politics: now you see it, now you don't. *Feminist Review* 5, 1–18.

Canguilhem, G. (1975) *Etudes d'Histoire et de Philosophie de Science*. Paris: Vrin.

Chalmers, A.F. (1976) *What is this Thing Called Science?* Milton Keynes: Open University Press.

Collinson, D. and Knights, D. (1986) 'Jobs for the boys': Sex discrimination in life insurance recruitment. *E.C.O. Research Bulletin* 9 (Spring), 24–44.

Cowie, E. (1978) Woman as sign. *m/f* 1, 49–64.

Cronbach, L. (1957) The two disciplines of scientific psychology. *American Psychologist* 12, 671–84.

Easlea, B. (1981) *Science and Sexual Oppression: Patriarchy's Confrontation with Woman and Nature*. London: Weidenfeld & Nicolson.

Easlea, B. (1983) *Fathering the Unthinkable: Masculinity, Scientists and the Nuclear Arms Race*. London: Pluto Press.

Eichler, M. (1980) *The Double Standard: A Feminist Critique of Feminist Social Science*. London: Croom Helm.

Filmer, P., Philipson, M., Silverman, D. and Walsh, D. (1972) *New Directions in Sociological Theory*. London: Collier Macmillan.

Foucault, M. (1977) *Discipline and Punish*. London: Allen Lane.

Foucault, M. (1979) *The History of Sexuality*. Vol. I: *An Introduction*. London: Allen Lane.

Frosh, S. (1987) *The Politics of Psychoanalysis*. London: Macmillan.

Giddens, A. (ed.) (1974) *Positivism and Sociology*. London: Macmillan.

Giddens, A. (1976) *New Rules of Sociological Method*. London: Macmillan.

Giddens, A. (1979) *Central Problems in Social Theory*. London: Macmillan.

Gilligan, C. (1982) *In a Different Voice: Psychological Theory and Women's Development*. Cambridge, MA: Harvard University Press.

Glaser, B.E. and Strauss, A.L. (1967) *The Discovery of Grounded Theory*. Chicago: Aldine.

Goldstein, A.P. and Krasner, L. (1987) *Modern Applied Psychology*. Oxford: Pergamon.

Goodall, K. (1972) Shapers at work. *Psychology Today* 6 (6), 62–3.

Goodfield, J. (1981) *An Imagined World*. New York: Harper & Row.

Grimshaw, J. (1986) *Feminist Philosophers: Women's Perspectives on Philosophical Traditions*. Brighton: Wheatsheaf.

Hartsock, N. (1979) Feminist theory and the development of revolutionary strategy. In Z. Eisenstein (ed.), *Capitalist Patriarchy and the Case for Socialist Feminism*. New York: Monthly Review Press.

Henriques, J., Hollway, W., Urwin, C., Venn, C. and Walkerdine, V. (1984) *Changing the Subject: Psychology, Social Relations and Subjectivity*. London: Methuen.

Herriot, P. and Wingrove J. (1984) Decision processes in graduate pre-selection. *Journal of Occupational Psychology* 57, 269–76.

Hollway, W. (1981) 'I just wanted to kill a woman.' Why? The Ripper and male sexuality. *Feminist Review* 9, 33–44. Reprinted in *Feminist Review* (ed.) (1987), *Sexuality: A Reader*. London: Virago.

Hollway, W. (1982) *Identity and Gender Difference in Adult Social Relations*. Unpublished Ph.D. thesis, University of London.

Hollway, W. (1984a) Gender difference and the production of subjectivity. In Henriques, J., Hollway, W., Urwin, C., Venn, C. and Walkerdine, V., *Changing the Subject: Psychology, Social Relations and Subjectivity*. London: Methuen.

Hollway, W. (1984b) Women's power in heterosexual sex. *Women's Studies International Forum* 7 (1), 63–8.

Hollway, W. (1986) WIP: Why a women-only organisation? *Newsletter of Women in Psychology* 1.

Hollway, W. (in preparation) *Origins and Development of Work and Organizational Psychology: The Production of the Individual at Work*. London: Sage.

Hunt, S.M. (1974) *Sex Differences*. Ithaca: Vernon Scott Assoc.

Jakobson, R. (1962) *Selected Writings*. The Hague: Mouton.

Itzin, C. (1986) Media images of women: the social construction of ageism and sexism. In S. Wilkinson (ed.), *Feminist Social Psychology*. Milton Keynes: Open University Press.

Journal of the National Institute of Psychology (1922) Unattributed report, p. 76.

Keller, E. Fox (1983) *A Feeling for the Organism: The Life and Work of Barbara McClintock*. New York: Freeman.

Keller, E. Fox (1985) *Reflections on Gender and Science*. London: Yale University Press.

Keller, E. Fox (1987) Learning about women: gender, politics and power. *Daedalus* (Fall), 77–91.

Klein, M. (1960) *Our Adult World and its Roots in Infancy*. London: Tavistock.

Lacan, J. (1977) *Ecrits: A Selection*. London: Tavistock.

Laplanche, J. and Pontalis, J.B. (1973) *The Language of Psychoanalysis*. London: Hogarth Press.

Lauer, R.H. and Handel, W.H. (1977) *Social Psychology: The Theory and Application of Symbolic Interactionism*. Boston, MA: Houghton Mifflin.

Levinson, D.J., Darrow, C., Klein, E., Levinson, M. and McKee, B. (1978) *Seasons of a Man's Life*. New York: Ballantine Books.

Levy, P. (1981) On the relation between method and substance in psychology. *Bulletin of the British Psychological Society* 34, 265-70.

Lloyd, G. (1984) *The Man of Reason: Male and Female in Western Philosophy*. London: Methuen.

McDougall, W. (1923) *An Outline of Psychology*. London: Methuen.

Mama, A. (1987) *Race and Subjectivity: A Study of Black Women*. Unpublished Ph.D. thesis, University of London. Published version forthcoming, Routledge.

Marshall, J. (1984) *Women Managers: Travellers in a Male World*. Chichester: Wiley.

Marshall, J. (1986) Experiences of women managers. In S. Wilkinson (ed.) *Feminist Social Psychology*. Milton Keynes: Open University Press.

Mischel, T. (ed.) (1977) *The Self: Psychological and Philosophical Issues*. Oxford: Basil Blackwell.

Mitchell, J. (ed.) (1986) *The Selected Melanie Klein*. Harmondsworth: Penguin.

Moorrees, V. and Northcott, C.H. (1933) Industrial psychology at Rowntree's cocoa works. *Human Factor* (May), 159–68.

Munsterberg, H. (1913) *Psychology and Industrial Efficiency*. Boston, MA: Houghton Mifflin.

Muscio, B. (1974) *Lectures in Industrial Psychology*. Easton: Hive. First published 1919.

Nicolson, P. (1986) Developing a feminist approach to depression following childbirth. In Wilkinson, S. (ed.), *Feminist Social Psychology*. Milton Keynes: Open University Press.

Packard, V. (1968) *The Sexual Wilderness*. London: Pan.

Parlee, M.B. (1979) Psychology and Women. *Signs* 5 (1), 121–33.

Potter, J. and Wetherell, M. (1987) *Discourse and Social Psychology: Beyond Attitudes and Behaviour*. London: Sage.

Reason, P. and Rowan, J. (1981) *Human Inquiry: A Sourcebook of New Paradigm Research*. Chichester: Wiley.

Riley, D. (1978) Developmental psychology, biology and Marxism. *Ideology and Consciousness* 4, 73–92.

Roethlisberger, J. (1954) *Training for Human Relations*. Cambridge, MA: Harvard University Press.

Roethlisberger, F.J. and Dickson, W.J. (1939) *Management and the Worker*. Cambridge, MA: Harvard University Press.

Rose, M. (1985) *Industrial Behaviour: Theoretical Development since Taylor*. Harmondsworth: Penguin.

Rose, N. (1985) *The Psychological Complex: Psychology, Politics and Society in England 1869–1939*. London: Routledge & Kegan Paul.

Rosenberg, B.G. and Sutton-Smith, B. (1972) *Sex and Identity*. New York: Holt, Rinehart & Winston.

Rotman, B. (1980) Mathematics: An Essay in Semiotics. University of Bristol, mimeo.

Sayers, J. (1983) *Biological Politics: Feminist and Anti-feminist Perspectives.* London: Tavistock.

Sayers, J. (1986) Sexual identity and difference: psychoanalytic perspectives. In S. Wilkinson (ed.), *Feminist Social Psychology*. Milton Keynes: Open University Press.

Schrödinger, E. (1967) *Mind and Matter*. New York Cambridge: Cambridge University Press.

Segal, H. (1981) *Introduction to the Work of Melanie Klein*. London: Hogarth Press.

Selby, J.M. (1984) Feminine Identity and Contradiction: Women Research Students at Cambridge University. Unpublished Ph.D. thesis, University of Cambridge.

Silverman, D. (1972) Methodology and meaning. In P. Filmer et al. (eds.), *New Directions in Sociological Theory*. London: Collier Macmillan.

Simmel, G. (1923) The relative and the absolute problem of the sexes. *On Women, Sexuality and Love*, 3rd edn, trans. Guy Oakes. New Haven: Yale University Press. First published 1911.

Spare Rib (1981) 104, letters.

Stanley, L. and Wise, S. (1983) *Breaking Out: Feminist Consciousness and Feminist Research*. London: Routledge & Kegan Paul.

Student Christian Movement (1966) *Sex and Morality: A Report presented to the British Council of Churches*. London: SCM Press.

Tajfel, H. (1972) Experiments in a Vacuum. In J.A. Israel and H. Tajfel (eds.), *The Context of Social Psychology*. London/San Diego: Academic Press.

Urwin, C. (1984) Power relations and the emergence of language. In Henriques, J., Hollway, W., Urwin, C., Venn, C. and Walkerdine, V., *Changing the Subject: Psychology, Social Relations and Subjectivity*. London: Methuen.

Venn, C. (1984) The subject of psychology. In Henriques, J., Hollway, W., Urwin, C., Venn, C. and Walkerdine, V. *Changing the Subject: Psychology, Social Relations and Subjectivity*. London: Methuen.

Viteles, M.S. (1933) *Industrial Psychology*. London: Cape.

Walkerdine, V. (1985) Dreams from an ordinary childhood. In L. Heron (ed.), *Truth, Dare or Promise*. London: Virago.

Walkerdine, V. (1986) Post-structuralist theory and everyday social practices. In S. Wilkinson (ed.), *Feminist Social Psychology*. Milton Keynes: Open University Press.

Walkerdine, V. (1988) *The Mastery of Reason: Cognitive Development and the Production of Rationality*. London: Routledge.

Watson, J.B. (1919) *Psychology from the Standpoint of a Behaviorist*. Philadelphia: Lippincott.

Weedon, C. (1987) *Feminist Practice and Poststructuralist Theory*. Oxford: Basil Blackwell.

Weinreich, H. (1978) Sex Role Socialisation. In J. Chetwynd and O. Hartnett (eds), *The Sex-Role System*. London: Routledge & Kegan Paul.

Wetherell, M. (1986) Linguistic repertoires and literary criticism: new directions for a social psychology of gender. In S. Wilkinson (ed.), *Feminist Social Psychology*. Milton Keynes: Open University Press.

Wilkinson, S. (ed.) (1986) *Feminist Social Psychology*. Milton Keynes: Open University Press.

Winnicott, D.W. (1964) *The Child, the Family and the Outside World*. London: Tavistock.

Index